Martin Luther
The Great Reformer

J. A. Mor...

Revised by Michael ...

Christian Liberty Press
Arlington Heights, Illinois

Originally published as:
Martin Luther: The Lion-hearted
St. Louis: Concordia Publishing House, 1910

Revised Edition
Copyright © 1994 Christian Liberty Press
2007 Printing

Christian Liberty Press

502 West Euclid Avenue
Arlington Heights, Illinois 60004
www.christianlibertypress.com

Cover design and graphics by Bob Fine
Layout and editing by Edward J. Shewan

The translation of Luther's preface to Romans (*Appendix*) was made by Bro. Andrew Thornton, OSB, for the Saint Anselm College Humanities Program. Copyright © 1983 by Saint Anselm Abbey.

ISBN 978-1-930092-16-7
        1-930092-16-4

Set in Trump Mediaeval

Printed in the United States of America

Contents

The Rallying Cry of the Great Reformers

Sola Gratia, Sola Fida, Solo Christo, Sola Scriptura, Soli Deo Gloria!

1. Sola Gratia   "Grace alone" This indicates that salvation is by grace alone. It is not by "works" but is solely by the unmerited favour of God.

2. Sola Fida   "Faith alone" This indicates saving grace is gifted to believers by God through faith alone - and this itself is the gift of God by the regenerating work of the Holy Spirit.

3. Solo Christo   "Christ alone" This indicates that the salvation which is by grace is through a faith in the person and "finished work" of Christ in redemption.

4. Sola Scriptura   "The Scriptures alone" This indicates that the believers faith is grounded in the Holy Scriptures - the revealed Word of God in the Bible. It is not based on Christian tradition or any other authority - nor any mixture of such.

5. Soli Deo Gloria   "The Glory of God alone" This indicates that all that we are and all that we do as believers is to be for God's glory alone—and this was and is His sovereign purpose in Creation and Redemption.

Introduction

Great heroes are inspiring examples that help spur us on to noble endeavor. While we do not want to follow men so blindly that we lose sight of the Christ of God, yet there is room for conforming to the injunction of the great apostle, who says, "Follow me as I follow Christ."

Luther followed Christ. He was not humanly perfect by any means—who of us is? But, he did the right as God gave him to see the right, and it mattered not whether it was prince or pauper who tried to divert him from his path of duty. He kept right on battling for the truth. His own indomitable character is reflected in that hymn, A Mighty Fortress Is Our God.

This biography presents the leading aspects of the life of Luther and the *Appendix* contains a choice example of one of Luther's writings. We trust this material will inspire our noble young people to follow Luther as he followed Christ. To this task it is committed.

Michael J. McHugh
Arlington Heights, Illinois
2003

Calvin held Luther in the deepest reverence, and gladly called himself his disciple. He called him "that illustrious apostle of Christ, through whose labors the purity of the gospel has been restored to this age."

Benjamin B. Warfield

Chapter 1

A Poor Boy

On November 10, 1483, when Hans and Margaret Luther laid glad eyes upon the face of their newborn son, they little thought or even dreamed that they were looking into the face of one who would not only change the destinies of nations, but who would change the aspect of human history for all time to come. It is said that every child is an unlocked chest of possibilities. On this memorable date of November 10, 1483, God presented these humble German peasant parents with a gifted soul that had a God-ordained destiny, the extent and value of which will not be known fully until all human achievements will be brought to account.

When a boy who has poverty for his companion is inclined to find fault with the company that he is forced to keep, he should comfort himself by reading about the boyhood days of Martin Luther—a son of poverty who by the strength of God and the grace of Christ, stamped his name on every page of history written subsequently to his day. Martin Luther did not inherit from his parents luxuries that money can buy, but he did inherit those sterling qualities of character that came into such good play when he was brought face to face with those battles that proved him a great victor. He inherited sturdiness of character, strong will-power, steadfastness of purpose, honesty of heart, and a religious disposition. He who falls heir to such should consider himself blessed of God and happy.

The Luthers were Germans. They lived in the Thuringian Mountains. If you will look at a map of Germany, you will find that these mountains are located near the central part of that country. Nestled among these steep and beautiful mountains is the little town of Eisleben. In it Martin Luther was born and here he died. The very next day after Martin was born, he was taken to the church and there baptized, for his parents were very religious people and they had been taught by their church that it was their duty as parents to have their children baptized as soon as possible.

Martin Luther was still a small baby when his parents moved from Eisleben to Mansfeld, where his father found work in the mines. The struggle to provide a living here for their loved ones was hard for Martin's parents. When he grew to be a man, he had this to say concerning those struggles: "My father was a poor miner and my mother carried the wood from the forests on her back; they both worked their flesh off their bones in order to bring up their children." And "bring" them up they did. Martin, his brother, and his three sisters were not permitted just to "grow up" and do as they pleased. The parents taught their children religion—in those days it was quite generally believed that religion could be most efficiently taught with the rod. Those were the days before the great religious Reformation, in which Luther was to have so large a part, had swept over the world. The then prevailing religion of Roman Catholicism was largely a religion based upon human traditions.

Luther's parents were devout Catholics and their strenuous and even unmerciful discipline of their children, they believed, was the very best for the children's welfare. Because Martin stole a nut one time, his mother whipped him until the blood flowed. His father punished him so severely, at another time, that Martin could stand it no longer and fled from home. However, when Luther had grown to be a man, he did not harbor any bitterness in his heart against his parents. He remembered their awful grind of self-sacrificing toil and knew that they had toiled because they desired to give them proper food, clothing, and education. In speaking of the severe punishments which he received from the hands of his parents, he remarked. "They meant it well from the depths of their hearts, but they did not know how to distinguish the dispositions to which punishment is to be adapted." In later life—when God had given him greater light regarding Biblical truth and when, through Him, this light had been shed over all Europe and even over all the world—he saw that the severity of his parents had only reflected the un-Biblical extremes that had pervaded their generation.

As I have said, Luther was taught religion in his boyhood home at Mansfeld; but such a religion as it was! It was a religion without balanced Biblical truth, and such religion is always bondage most grievous. His mother gathered the children around her knees and told them of the Father and Christ. But what sort of ideas of God and Christ did Luther get in those hours of early piety? Hear what he says in later life about it:

"From early childhood I was accustomed to turn pale and tremble whenever I heard the name of Christ mentioned, for I was taught to look upon him as a stern and wrathful judge. We were taught that we ourselves had to atone for our sins, and since we could not make sufficient amends or do acceptable works, our teachers directed us to the saints in heaven, and made us to call upon Mary the mother of Christ and implore her to avert from us Christ's wrath, and make him inclined to be merciful to us." The Luthers, in accordance with the times in which they lived, believed in all sorts of supernatural influences. Luther says that in his childhood he had constant dread of witches and demons, which he believed always haunted his pathway or hid in dark corners to seize upon him as he passed. The Thuringian Forest, which surrounded the town, was supposed to be

The Roman Catholic Mass

teeming with evil spirits, and beneath the ground, in the mines where Luther's father worked, was a possible dwelling place of the devil himself. Superstitious fears thus fastened themselves upon his mind, and he had no liberty until he found it in a saner conception of the boundless love and limitless power of Christ. Such was the religious atmosphere which young Luther breathed. Such were the gruesome thoughts that haunted him by night and taunted him by day. Is it any wonder that a merciful God poured the light of Truth into his soul, and that the light which could dispel the darkness of that soul could also lighten the path of millions of others who sat in darkness?

Chapter 2

School Days

Martin's father longed to give his children better educational advantages than he himself had enjoyed. As Martin was the eldest son, they were especially desirous that he be well trained. Of course, strictly speaking, Martin's training began in the home at his mother's knee, but while he was still of a tender age, his ambitious parents started him in the village school. It seems that Luther attended this school more or less regularly until he was thirteen years of age. When Luther met with severity in his home from the hand of his parents, that severity was mellowed with an honest love. But when the timid, barefoot boy stepped over the threshold of the village school he found himself in different hands. Here he met severity without love. Doubtless Luther had some good teachers in school, but frequently, he suffered at the hands of those who were brutal and ignorant. He received fifteen whippings at school during one morning. This was not because he was so wicked, but because his teacher was ignorant. The lower schools throughout Germany at that time were hardly worthy of the name "school," and Luther compared them to "hell and purgatory."

The young Martin Luther did not appreciate such a school, but he was not allowed to quit, for his parents had an honest ambition that he should be educated to become a lawyer. In this direction they bent every effort, but they were greatly disappointed, as we shall see later, when Luther decided to leave all worldly occupations to enter upon a strictly religious life. So Luther went on to the village school, studied his Latin, received his whippings, and hated his teachers until he was thirteen years of age. It is a wonder that he did not become disgusted with teachers, books, and beating-rods and then run away from home and become an outlaw. Think what it would have meant to the world if he had done so. But perhaps, in these trying days, he read the life of some great man as you are doing, and his soul must have been set ablaze with an ambition to become educated and good, so that he might be able to accomplish something of worth in the world. Therefore, he continued his studies. It is easy to imagine that young Luther had two burning ambitions—one to become wise and the other to become good—because he later became both, and he could hardly have become so without such ambitions. If a young man would find the greatest blessing in the world, let him go in search of righteousness; if he would find the next greatest blessing in the world, let his search be for knowledge. Luther sought and found them both. If a young man would shun the greatest curse in the world, let him shun sin; if he would shun the next greatest curse in the world, let him shun ignorance. As a young man, Luther worked hard to shun both.

When the schoolmasters at Mansfeld were through pounding Latin into Luther with a stick, he was ready for a well-earned promotion. So about the time that Columbus was getting ready to make his third trip to America, Luther was getting ready to make his first trip to school away from home. This trip of Luther's took him to Magdeburg, a town located on the Elbe River about forty miles from his home. He was accompanied to Magdeburg by another lad from Mansfeld. Little is known as to what subjects the reformer-to-be studied while at Magdeburg, but more is known as to how he paid his expenses. The school that Luther attended at Magdeburg was a religious school managed by pious persons who exacted no tuition of Luther, because of his poverty. Young Luther, though freed from tuition expense, was confronted with the problem of meeting his personal expenses by starting with an empty purse. However, when a young man is determined to have an education he generally gets it even though he has to conquer poverty to do so. Though poor in purse, Luther was rich in natural gifts. He had a good pair of legs to carry him from house to house and a strong voice to sing when he arrived. It was common, during his stay in Magdeburg, to see him with a group of fellow students as poor as himself, standing at the front gate of a wealthy citizen. Sometimes they were invited to come in, sit at the table, and eat with those to whom they sang. Sometimes with eager hands, they received "handouts" at the door. The young student of the present day, who has to do janitorial work or wash dishes in order to pay his school expenses, should extract comfort from the fact that he is following in the footprints of one of the world's greatest figures—only he uses his hands; whereas, Luther used his lungs.

During his stay in Magdeburg, Luther was profoundly impressed with the strict piety that prevailed in connection with school-life there. Thirty-five years after he had attended this school he wrote:

> When, in my fourteenth year, I went to school at Magdeburg, I saw with my own eyes a prince of Anhalt ... who went in a friar's cowl[†] on the highway to beg bread, and carried a sack, like a donkey, so heavy that he bent under it, but his companion walked by him without a burden; this prince alone might serve as an example of the grisly, shorn holiness of the world. They had so stunned him that he did all the works of the cloister like any other brother, and he had so fasted, watched, and mortified his flesh, that he looked like a death's head, mere skin and bones; indeed he soon after died, for he could not long bear such a sever life. In short, whoever looked at him had to gasp for pity and must needs be ashamed of his own worldly position."

Luther had seen the prince he here describes in the days when his boyish mind was filled with the philosophy of the ascetic. In those days, he had been taught and led to believe that the favor of God was secured by physical self-abasement. To behold such an example would naturally impress him with the thought that this prince had a high degree of righteousness.

---

† A *cowl* is a long-hooded garment worn by a monk.

When Luther had sung in the streets and studied in the school at Magdeburg for scarcely one year, his stay in that city came to an end. Eisenach was a city twenty-five miles farther from Luther's home than was Magdeburg. In that city was a school known as the School of St. George. This was the native town of Martin's mother, and she had a relative living there, named Hutter. Perhaps Mrs. Luther had hopes that her son, Martin, could live with this relative and thus, avoid the necessity of begging his way as he was forced to do in Magdeburg. In this she was mistaken, for Martin had no sooner landed in the city than the clear notes of his song were lifted on the breeze of the morning; and there he begged bread for his body while in search of "bread" for his mind. Doubtless he became very much downcast at times. He may even have been tempted to return home to Mansfeld to go into the dark mines and there spend his life toiling beside his father; yet that would have been a long and dreary song that had no ending. One day, however, Martin's singing did come to a happy termination.

In the city of Eisenach lived a woman of beautiful character—Ursula Cotta. She had often seen the poor Luther boy in the streets and had heard the clear note of his song. She had eyes that saw and a heart that pities. She saw in the neglected boy qualities of great worth and she pitied him in his poverty. She and her husband, Conrad, invited the poor lad to come into their beautiful home and share its comforts. This event was the dawning of a new and bright day in Luther's life. It was the first time in all his career, that he had felt the soft touch of refined sympathy. He spent about four years in this stately old house, which is still standing and visited annually by thousands of people who know of the great work of the Reformer and who bless the memory of the woman who helped him in his hour of deep need.

Luther's stay in the city of Eisenach was indeed a happy one. He referred to the city in later life as "that dear city." He entered heart and soul into his studies in the school of St. George. He stored his mind with rich gems of thought and drank deeply of the spirit of piety possessed by his teachers. In this school, Martin came into contact with the great currents of thought that were being poured forth by the intellectuals as a result of their researches into old and neglected libraries and museums.

At the close of his four years' happy residence in the Cotta home, Luther made preparation to enter the famous university of Erfurt, about twenty miles east of Eisenach. By this time his father at Mansfeld, by reason of hard labor and simple honesty, had brought himself to a place of comparative financial and social comfort. He had been placed in one of the highest offices of the village. He was still ambitious for the educational success of his son and gave him all possible assistance in entering the great university. About May of 1501, Luther enrolled as a student at Erfurt. It seems that he remained at this center of learning for about four years, during which time he threw himself ambitiously into a study of the curriculum provided by the university. Not a great deal is known of the life of the future reformer during his university days. He lived a life of strict morality and suffered somewhat from depression and some illness. In 1502, he took the degree of bachelor of arts and three years later that of master of arts.

After Luther had left the lower school in Mansfeld, he spent about nine years in training before he entered upon what he at that time supposed to be his life's work—that of a monk. He was able to use the information gained in these years of schooling later in life, when he was called upon to combat the works and workers of unrighteousness in high places.

Chapter 3

A Great Battle

The life of Luther was a life of battles. Perhaps he never shouldered a musket, unsheathed a sword, or operated a machine gun, but his weapons of warfare were not carnal. The greatest battles of life are fought within one's own soul. From early childhood Luther had been haunted by fears that God's wrath was being stored up against him. He felt sure that God was angry with him, and he lived in constant dread of the judgment day. Now, during the latter years of his university career, he was afraid that he might die suddenly and then he would be eternally damned. "What must I do to be saved?" was the question of questions in his heart. If he had ever read the Bible with proper understanding, the answer would have come sweet and clear, "Believe on the Lord Jesus Christ, Luther, and you shall be saved." Nevertheless, the Bible to him was a closed book. He read it more or less, but like Saul of Tarsus, he was blinded by the scales on his eyes. He did not look to the Bible for an answer to his burning question. He had been taught to look to the Roman Catholic Church for the answer. The church replied, "Do good works, do penance, humiliate yourself, shut yourself away from the world as much as possible, and you shall be saved." Luther believed the Church. It advised him to become a monk if he would be perfect and have great reward in heaven.

But what is a monk? A monk in Luther's day was a man who had become so good (according to his own idea of goodness) that he was good for nothing. He was a man who had retired from secular life to give himself entirely to religious duties. This religious work was to be centered upon himself. He was to make himself holy, not by faith in Jesus, by which one serves his fellow men and tries to bring others to Jesus, but by prayers, fastings, and self-humiliation. He was to vow that he would not marry, that he would remain in poverty, and that he would obey the rules of the monkish order to which he belonged. He was supposed to live in a monastery with other monks as useless to his fellow men as himself, and to spend his days in keeping himself fit to go to heaven when he died. All of this is what the Church told Martin Luther he must do to be saved. Luther, of course, wanted to be saved, but he did not see how all this would bring him salvation. So here is where the battle began.

All through his years in the university, this struggle went on in his heart. "What must I do to be saved?" "Shall I be lost forever, or shall I obey the voice of the church?" "Shall I give up hopes of a brilliant career in secular life?" "Shall I become a monk and be scoffed at by all my young university associates, and bring down upon my youthful head the hot wrath of my poor old father, who has worked so hard that I might have an education?" All of these questions, with others equally baffling, surged through his mind.

When Luther was in the midst of this struggle, certain happenings in Erfurt seemed to warn him that he was near the gates of eternity. The plague broke out in the city; many of the students died, and others, panic-stricken, fled from the place. In the face of these happenings, Luther became more solemn than ever. He tried to listen to the professors of law lecture, but their lectures were insufferably dry and uninteresting to him. What did he care for the long, drawn-out discourses of technical law when his soul was yearning for an assurance that it was saved? He left the university and went home, perhaps for the purpose of persuading his father to let him give up his study of law. We have no reason, however, to believe that his father consented.

On July 2, as he was returning to the university, he was overtaken by a severe thunderstorm. The rain came down in torrents, the wind blew hard and the thunder roared, and angry streaks of lightning flashed. The young master of philosophy was stricken with horror. He thought the devil was actually after him. If it seems strange that a university student should get frightened at a thunderstorm, we have only to recall that a belief in the direct intervention of Satan was prominent in the thought of that day. Luther fell on his face and prayed, not to God, but to St. Anna; for he believed that he could not come directly to the heavenly Father in his prayers, but that some departed saint must intercede for him. Here he made a vow that he would become a monk. The battle was over.

A few days later, he invited a group of his fellow students to a social gathering. Here they feasted, sang, and had a jolly good time. Young Luther seemed to enjoy himself immensely with his friends, among whom he was a favorite; for he was a young man of high intellectuality, and many pleasing qualities. In the midst of the fun, he broke the news of his decision to his friends in these words: "Friends, today you see me for the last time; I have decided to become a monk." They thought he was joking. When they were finally assured that he was in dead earnest, they did everything in their power to pull him away from his purpose; but they were unsuccessful.

That very night, he went to the monastery where he disappeared behind the great cloister doors. The monastery, which Luther entered, was conducted by the Augustinian order of friars. There were several others in Erfurt. Luther entered this one because it had a reputation for being the best. If it were the best, pity the

worst! Luther had not been in this place very long until he found that some of the monks were not in any sense good people. Some, like Luther, doubtless had entered the monastery in the hope of becoming good. But many of them, instead of growing good, had grown worse and were not ashamed of it. Some were idle, gluttonous and lazy—enormous fellows with red noses, showing that they were more interested in wine and sausages than in honoring God. Some of these impious monks made life miserable for Luther. They scoffed at his serious concern for his soul.

Luther was sent by the authorities of the monastery into the streets of the city to beg. As he had grown weary of begging during his school days at Magdeburg and Eisenach, he did not relish it here. But there were two reasons, according to the fat monks' way of thinking, why he should comply. First, his begging brought a supply of eatables to those in the monastery. Second, it helped Luther to be humble. It, according to the monks, brought a physical blessing to the monks and a spiritual blessing to Luther himself.

The monastery's dismal life undermined Luther's health. He refused to eat, until he wasted away and became mere skin and bones. Finally, the vicar-general, or manager of the cloister, Staupitz, who was a kindly German, noticed Luther's sad condition and took an interest in him. He encouraged Luther to trust Jesus as his Savior; telling him that God was not angry with him, but that Luther was angry with himself. Later Luther wrote, "If Dr. Staupitz, or rather God through Dr. Staupitz, had not helped me out of my trials I would have drowned in them and would have been in hell long ago."

When Luther's father heard that he had become a monk, his wrath knew no bounds. He did everything in his power to persuade his son to leave off such a course, but to no avail. Martin was ordained a priest in February 1507. When he celebrated his first mass in May of that year, he invited his father to attend. Luther's father came, with some of his friends, and presented his son with a beautiful present. It seems that by this time, he had softened somewhat—but not altogether. Martin thought to take advantage of this occasion and tried to explain to his father that he had chosen a wise and noble course; but his father only replied, "Have you not heard that a man should honor his parents?"

Up at Wittenberg, about seventy miles east and about sixty miles north of Erfurt, was a new university. It had been founded about six years previously by the Elector of Saxony for the purpose of teaching the philosophy of Aristotle. Wittenberg was a much smaller and less attractive town than handsome Erfurt,

Elector Frederick III of Saxony

but it was to be a prominent name in the world's history. About a year and a half after he was ordained as a priest, Luther was invited to this new university of Wittenberg to become a lecturer on moral philosophy.

The young priest named Martin took the call to teach at the University of Wittenberg. He soon arrived to take up his new duties as lecturer with renewed zeal and an optimistic spirit.

Climbing the Stairs of the Sancta Sanctorum in Rome

Chapter 4

A Sad Disappointment

While Martin Luther was lecturing at Wittenberg University, there came a happy day into his life. It happened as follows: there arose a dispute between several monasteries over which Staupitz had charge. The dispute grew fiercer, until it became plain that someone must go to Rome to lay the matter before the Pope for his decision. Luther—being a man of acute mentality, powerful language, and talent for discussion; and one who could be relied upon to carry a clear and honest report to the Pope and bring a similar report from him—received the appointment to accompany the agent of the aggrieved monasteries, John von Mecheln of Nuremberg. But what did Rome mean to the devout Catholic of Luther's day? To him, the name of Rome stood for everything that was worthy, good, and holy. Rome was the habitation of His Holiness the Pope. It was the hub and center of nearly everything pious.

It must have been, with a joyous heart, that Luther and his companion set out for Rome on a beautiful day in October, in the year 1510. However, the trip from Erfurt, Germany, to Rome, Italy, proved to be very difficult. It was not just a few hours' pleasant ride in a comfortable vehicle over smooth roads. No, indeed, it was a long, hard journey of several hundred miles over rugged mountains, across swollen streams, and through dismal swamps. They walked each step in single file. At one time during the trip, they were in very bad circumstances because their food ran out. Luther feared that they might never live to view the holy sights in Rome. In later years, he related the incident in these words:

> On the journey to Rome, the brother, with whom I was traveling, and I were very tired one night and slept with open windows until about six o'clock. When we awoke, our heads were full of vapors, so that we could only go four or five miles that day tormented by thirst and yet sickened by the wine and desiring only the water which is deadly there. At length, we were refreshed by two pomegranates—excellent fruit with which God saved our lives.

Although the journey was long and hard, and though the travelers were weary and footsore, Luther's pious heart was encouraged by the thought that if they kept it up, he would be repaid for all his hardships when his glad eyes would at last view the Holy City. After several weeks of this tiresome journey over mountains and plains and through cities and towns, they beheld, from the summit of a nearby hill, the domes and spires of the far-famed city on the River Tiber. The sight was almost more than Luther's religious heart could stand. He fell on his face to the ground, and exclaimed, "Hail, Holy Rome!" Just a few miles more and he actually placed his glad feet on the streets of the Eternal City.

Luther spent four weeks in seeing the sites of the great city. They were not four weeks of pure joy, as he had imagined that they might be. He had dreamed of the city as a city of saints. He had a wonderful idea of the holiness of Rome. Here was the seat of the pope, who was supposed to represent Christ, on earth. Here were the buildings, the streets, and other places made sacred by the patronage of saints. Instead of finding the city filled with an atmosphere of holiness and piety, as he had expected to find it, he found an atmosphere of worldliness and even vice. He heard stories of the very corrupt life of Alexander VI, who had been pope until about seven years before Luther's visit. He heard priests and others, high in church circles, speak lightly of things that the church held sacred. They even poked fun at those who were trying to live holy lives. All this caused Luther's heart to bow down with grief, and when he left Rome to go back to his home in Germany, he could scarcely bear up under his disappointment. He quoted a current saying. "If there is a hell, Rome is built over it."

When in the Holy City, Luther was very anxious to visit the chapel Sancta Sanctorum, in which was a flight of twenty-eight stairsteps. These steps were said to have been taken from the judgment hall of Pilate, in Jerusalem. Devout Catholics thought it a very religious thing to climb these steps. They thought it would make them good, and assure forgiveness of sins. Hundreds of thousands of people from different parts of the world had dragged themselves up this staircase on their knees. In the ninth century, Pope Leo IV had promised the forgiveness of nine years of sins for every step the pilgrim would climb on his knees. The pilgrim was to repeat certain prayers as he climbed. Martin Luther, in all probability, felt sure that this meritorious act would give him peace of soul. So (according to the account, as related later by Luther's son, Paul), on his knees he started up, but as he went up he did not feel any better. He had enough common sense, when it dawned on him, to realize that merely climbing stairsteps would not and could not take away his sins. As he was slowly dragging up those famous steps, something kept ringing in his ears. What was it? It was a passage of Scripture that he had read when he was lecturing on the Bible in the university at Wittenberg. The verse is found in the Book of Romans and reads, "The just shall live by faith." This Scripture brought a light into the soul of Luther that was to be shed over the whole world. It was God speaking to a needy soul. When Luther heard this voice, he was finished with climbing holy stairsteps on his knees. He was beginning to see that faith in Jesus Christ and His divine power will save and bring peace to the soul, when climbing so-called "holy steps" fails.

The whole world should feel indebted to God for raising up men like Luther to bring to light the great doctrine of salvation by faith. "Save yourself by good works," had been the cry for many generations! To be sure, Luther granted that good works were important. However, works were not enough. There was nothing in making holy pilgrimages and in kissing the pope to save a poor sinner. If he climbs holy stairsteps until exhausted, he still remains a sinner. If a sinner is to gain salvation, and thereby life eternal, he must do so through living faith in the blood of the crucified Savior. "Faith! Faith! Faith!" was Luther's cry. It was through living faith that this monk found peace to his own troubled soul; and it was the lost doctrine of faith in Christ that he restored to the world.

Since the days when Luther walked among men and experienced the glorious liberty of God's children by faith alone, millions of weary pilgrims have been led to the same truth. As we shall soon note, the life-changing message that God alone is the Author and Finisher of the faith in which His people live, was one which Luther believed was necessary for the church to boldly proclaim to every creature.

*The Castle Church
at Wittenberg*

*Luther nails
his Ninety-Five
Theses to the
door of the
Castle Church*

Chapter 5

An Act That Startled
the World

Luther had been a lecturer at Wittenberg University before he made the journey to Rome, but he was not made a regular professor until his return. The University was still a rather new institution, having been founded in 1502 by Frederick, called the Wise, who was elector or ruler of that part of Germany. A short while after his return from Rome, Luther became professor of theology in this new university. He considered this his main work. Luther was constantly learning. He put in a great deal of time in hard study, but he was also a man of the people. He took active part in practical, religious, and social questions of the times, and tried to use his learning for the betterment of these departments of life. This proved a great blessing to Luther, as well as to others. When we help others to happiness, we help ourselves to peace; hence, it seems that during Luther's work as a professor, the struggles of his own soul came to an end. He learned to trust in Jesus as his Savior and Lord.

Just whether or not he was converted at this time, we may not be able to say; perhaps he had the true faith before this time, but, nevertheless, he seems to have reached a place where he understood more about the abounding love of God. It was during this period that he wrote to a brother in the church:

> I should be very glad to know what is the state of your soul. Have you learned to despise your own righteousness and put your trust in the righteousness of Christ alone? Many do not know the righteousness of God which is given us abundantly and freely in Christ, but they endeavor to do good works and depend on their own effort, their own virtues, their own merits. You were full of this great error when you were here, and I was full of it. Even now I must fight against it, and I have not finished. Therefore, my beloved brother, learn Christ and Him crucified. Learn to despair of thyself and to say to Him, "Thou, Lord Jesus, art my righteousness, but I am thy sin. Thou hast assumed what was mine, and given me what was thine."

While Luther was a professor at the University of Wittenberg, there came to the next town a strange preacher, or perhaps we should call him a peddler rather than a preacher. His name was John Tetzel. He was an agent of the Pope of Rome. The Pope was building a great church in the Holy City and needed more money than was coming in the regular way; so he sent Tetzel up into Germany to sell indulgences everywhere. He gathered up great piles of money in this way for the Pope, and of course, he kept plenty for himself. Great crowds of people attended his meetings and gladly poured out their money for the indulgences. But what were indulgences? They were promises of the pope to forgive sins. For instance, if a man had committed so many sins, he could pay a certain amount of money and those sins would be forgiven. The indulgence was simply a written statement of this forgiveness. As Tetzel wanted to get all the money he could, he offered indulgences, not only for the sins the people had already committed, but also for those sins which they should commit in the future. Not only so, but a man could pay so much money for his dead relatives to be rescued from purgatory, the supposed place of temporary punishment.

Tetzel claimed to be a wonderful man. He said that he was even much greater than St. Peter himself. He told the people that, as soon as their money rattled in the collection chest, their friends were lifted out of purgatory. So it would be a hard-hearted fellow, indeed, who would not throw in a few coins to save a poor dead friend or relative from torment. Tetzel used burning words in picturing to the poor the tortures of those in

The sale of Indulgences

purgatory; and he bewailed the sheer meanness of a man who was not kind-hearted enough to pay a little money to save a soul from such torture. Of course, it would be unfair to say that all Catholics believed in such a corrupt way to get money. It is well known that Tetzel was a man unworthy even of the Roman Catholic religion.

When Martin Luther heard of the high-handed doing of this Tetzel, his pious soul was filled with righteous indignation. He determined to do what he could to keep the poor people from being deceived and robbed of their money. He longed that the people might know the truth, for by this time he had learned that it is truth, not tradition, that makes people free. This is when Luther wrote out his famous Ninety-Five Theses. These theses were simply written propositions, or statements questioning or condemning certain beliefs and practices of the church. They virtually denied the power of the pope to forgive sin. They condemned Tetzel's method of selling indulgences, and declared that the people should be taught that, if the Pope knew of the extortions of the preachers of indulgences, he would rather the great church, which was being built at Rome with indulgence money, be in ashes than be paid for in such a manner.

On October 31, 1517, there was a great gathering of the people at Wittenberg. It was on the day preceding what was known as the Feast of All Saints. A crowd of people had already gathered to look upon a collection of sacred relics which the Elector had gathered and which were displayed at this festival. At noon of this day preceding the Feast, Luther walked to the Wittenberg church and nailed a set of his Ninety-Five Theses to the wooden church door.

This day may be said to be the day when the great Protestant Reformation began. Of course, for many years in different countries of Europe the principle of reformation had been taking hold; but now the issue became clear-cut in Germany, and people began to take sides either for or against the lion-hearted reformer. When Luther walked to the church that day and tacked up his statements, he never dreamed of what a stir they would cause. He merely meant that they should be read by those who could understand Latin, for they were written in that language. He intended that these statements should be debated in the university. He little thought that the common crowd at Wittenberg would take such an interest in them. However, that paper on the church door expressed the very same feeling that existed, not only in Luther's mind, but also in the minds of tens of thousands of people in Germany, and in all Europe. Those who could read them in Latin explained them to those who could not understand Latin. Soon the news flew everywhere that there was a German professor at Wittenberg, who was bold enough to oppose the church. Several groups began to make copies of Luther's writings in the German language. Within four weeks, the news had reached Pope Leo X at Rome, and soon Luther's name was a household word in all Europe.

Papal Bull against Luther

Chapter 6

What the Pope Thought of Luther

When Pope Leo heard about the theses, he was not at all alarmed. However, he was very much disgusted. When he had read a copy of them, he remarked, "Oh, some drunken German has written them; as soon as he is sober again he will speak differently." Luther's friends were aware of the grave danger into which he was thrown. They knew the spirit of Rome. They remembered how that just about twenty years before this time, Savonarola had met his death in Italy, because he was bold enough to denounce Pope Alexander VI for his sins. They begged Luther to be a little more considerate of what he said. Even his former instructors in the University of Erfurt turned against him and reproached him for his insolent attacks upon the church. Some of the officials of the University begged him not to bring the institution into disgrace by giving it a reputation for being untrue to the doctrines of the church.

John Tetzel was given the doctor's degree by a neighboring university, and honors were heaped upon him in many quarters, which were done in testimony of the contempt that was held in those quarters for the reformer. Luther's courage did not fail. He believed he was doing God's will, and he refused to be persuaded by his friends or frightened by his foes into giving up the work which he felt called upon to do.

Finally, Pope Leo spoke. He ordered Luther to come to Rome within sixty days to answer to the charge of teaching unsound doctrine. Before Luther could decide whether to go or not, Cardinal Cajetan, who represented the Pope in the German Empire, warned Leo that there was danger in allowing Luther at large any longer. He requested that Luther be dealt with at once, at Augsburg. Cajetan was informed that he should arrest Luther immediately.

The trial was set to be held in Augsburg before a court of the Romish representatives. Cardinal Cajetan had instructions to use all diligence to see that the bold monk was brought to punishment if he did not recant. He was instructed to threaten with punishment, not only Luther himself, but all who would dare to house, shield, or in any way either openly or privately, protect, assist, or counsel the said Martin Luther.

When it became known to Luther that he must go to Augsburg to face the charges brought against him, it appears that he thought he would never return alive. "I must die," he said; and "Oh, the disgrace that I heap upon my poor parents!" But, "The Lord's will be done. Even at Augsburg, even in the midst of his enemies, Christ reigns. Let Christ live; let Luther die!" He was accompanied at Augsburg by Dr. Staupitz, and other friends, and he was guaranteed a safe-conduct by the Emperor Maximilian. When he reached Augsburg, in the month of October, he found that the council had adjourned, and most of the members departed. However, he had a meeting with Cardinal Cajetan.

The Cardinal talked to him with great courtesy at first, in the hope of getting him to apologize to the church and to the Pope. Luther replied that he was ready to apologize as soon as he was shown wherein he was wrong. The Cardinal said that in one of his theses, Luther had claimed that the treasury of the Church consisted not of the sufferings and merits of Christ. And in his Resolutions, or explanations of his theses, he had claimed that the sacrament or Lord's Supper, was of value only to those who had faith in the promise of God. He asked Luther to admit that he was wrong. Luther refused. The Cardinal became furious and shouted, "Go away! Revoke or do not come again before my eyes." He remarked to Dr. Staupitz, "I will no longer dispute with that beast, for it has deep eyes and wonderful speculations in its head." Luther slipped out of Augsburg by night, and made his way back to

Wittenberg arriving there October 30, just one day less than a year from the day he had nailed his Ninety-Five Theses to the church-door. The enraged Cardinal demanded that Luther should be sent in chains to Rome, but Frederick the Elector, who was determined that Luther should have a fair trial, would not allow that he be sent to Rome.

If Cardinal Cajetan was not smooth enough to fix things up with the "beast of Wittenberg," as he called Luther, the Pope had another agent who was much smoother, and he would send him to Germany to see what could be done. This was Charles von Miltitz, who was an old resident of Rome and thoroughly familiar with her ways. He was shrewd and cultured. He soon found that there was a tremendous sentiment, in Germany, in favor of Luther's movement. He said that three persons out of every four he met were on Luther's side. Of course, he was too wise to disregard this sentiment of the common people. He had a meeting with Luther and talked matters over with him. He denounced Tetzel as a fraud, and agreed that Luther's case should be tried by an enlightened bishop. It was agreed by him and Luther that both sides should keep silent, and let the trouble between Luther and the Church die out. Luther agreed to write a letter to the Pope and apologize, if he had been too rough in what he had said. Miltitz was also to write to the Pope, and tell him that an adjustment had been made. So it seemed that the trouble was settled.

Luther meant to keep his word when he promised to keep quiet, and it was not his fault that he did not. Perhaps it is well that he was drawn further into the discussion, for had he remained silent perhaps we never

would have had the great spiritual Reformation that shook the whole world. In the University of Wittenberg was a professor called Carlstadt, who was a friend of Luther's, and a believer in his doctrines. In the University of Ingolstadt was a professor named Eck. In Eck's reply, it was very plain that while he was claiming to attack Carlstadt, he in reality was attacking Luther. Luther protested that it was unfair for him to be required to keep silent when his enemies were allowed to rage. He immediately published some new theses in opposition to Eck, which brought on the debate at Leipzig. This debate lasted for three weeks. Carlstadt proved to be no match for Dr. Eck, but Luther came boldly forward the second week and defended the truth in the very face of those who were its enemies. In this debate, it became clear that the breach between Luther and the Roman Catholic Church was growing wider and wider.

In 1520, Luther wrote his famous Address to the German Nobility. This was an appeal to the German people to stand for their national rights. It called attention to the fact that the German nation was overridden by the lords of Rome and called upon them to rise and throw off their yoke of bondage. He said it would be well if ninety-nine parts of the papal court were done away and called it, "a swarm of vermin yonder in Rome" and "ravening wolves in sheep's clothing." He said in this address that the Romanists had built *three walls* about themselves, behind which they carried on their mischief. Luther declared his intention to hammer these three walls down and reveal the spiritual poverty of the popes and their colleagues. The **first wall** was the pope's claim that he and his emissaries were not subject to the temporal power. If threatened with the law for their misdeeds, they said that the law could not touch them; for they were higher than any temporal power and were not subject to it. Strange belief to hold, we say today, but in Luther's day almost everybody held that belief. It had been taught for years, and even for centuries. But Luther declared that all Christians were on an equal footing in this respect, and that all were alike, subject to the temporal power. Crime should be punished by the temporal power whether the criminal were pope, priest, or peasant. In his Address to the Nobility, he stated that there is no difference among Christians save of office alone.

To make the subject clearer, he gave this illustration:

> Let us say that a little company of Christian laymen were taken prisoner and carried away to a desert island. Since they had among them no priest consecrated by a bishop, they agreed to choose one of them, married or unmarried, and were to order him to baptize, to celebrate the mass, to absolve, and to preach.

This man would be as truly a priest as though all the bishops and all the popes had consecrated him.

A priest, therefore, said Luther, is nothing in Christendom but an official. As long as he holds his office he has precedence over others; if he be deprived of it, he is a peasant or townsman like the rest. Thus a cobbler, a smith, a peasant, every man has the office and function of his calling; and yet all alike, they are consecrated priests and bishops. Every man in his work must be useful and beneficial to the rest.

Continuing, he stated that to say the temporal authority, being inferior to the clergy, dare not punish them, is as though one were to say that the hand may not help when the eye is suffering. Inasmuch as the temporal power has been ordained of God for the punishment of the bad and the protection of the good, we must let it do its duty throughout the whole Christian body without respect of persons, whether it strike pope, bishops, priests, monks, nuns, or anybody else. He raised the question that if a priest is killed, the country is burdened with severe and restrictive sanctions—why not, also, if a peasant is killed?

So Luther crumbled the first wall. Now for the **second wall**. This second wall, that the Romanists had built around themselves to shield them in their meanness, was the idea that the pope was the only one who could interpret the Scripture correctly. If a pope or a priest did any evil and was threatened by the Scriptures, it was easy enough for the pope to interpret the Bible in a way to suit himself. When his Holiness said a certain scripture meant a certain thing, everybody must keep silent, for according to the generally accepted theory, he could not make a mistake. So the

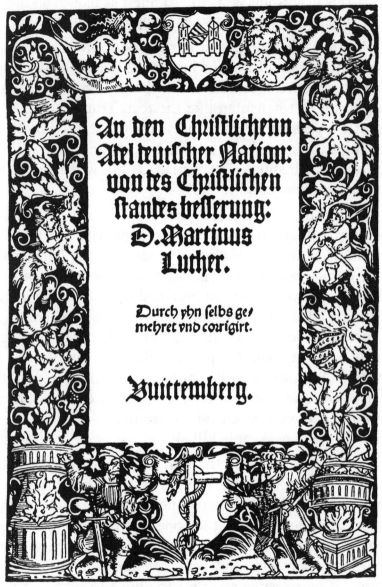

Luther's "Address to the Nobility"

people kept silent and the pope kept sinning. But Luther would not keep silent. He spent months and months in searching the Scriptures and reading church history. The more he searched and read, the more he believed that the whole idea of the pope's infallibility was a sham and a fraud. Listen to what he says:

> The second wall is still more flimsy and worthless. They wish to be the only masters of the Holy Scriptures, even though in all their lives they learn little from them. They assume for themselves sole authority, and with insolent juggling of words they would persuade us that the pope, whether he be a bad man or a good man, cannot err in matters of faith; and yet they cannot prove a single letter of it...." The Scriptures plainly teach that all Christians have the responsibility and privilege to study the Word of God.

> But not to fight them with mere words, we will quote the Scriptures. St. Peter says in 2 Peter 1:19–21: "We have also a more sure word of prophecy; Whereunto ye do well that ye take heed, as unto a light that shineth in a dark place, until the day dawn, and the daystar arise in your hearts: Knowing this first, that no prophecy of the Scripture is of any private interpretation. For the prophecy came not in old time by the will of man: but holy men of God spake as they were moved by the Holy Ghost." Indeed, the Book of Acts, Chapter 17, gives honor to those early believers in Thessalonica because they received the Word of God with readiness of mind, and searched the Scriptures diligently each day to verify whether what they were hearing was true or not.

> They must confess that there are pious Christians among us, who have the true faith, Spirit, understanding, Word, and mind of Christ. Why, then, should we reject their word and understanding, and follow the pope, who has neither faith nor Spirit? ... Balaam's ass also was wiser than the prophet himself. If God thus spoke by an ass against a prophet, why should he not be able even now to speak by a righteous man against the pope?

So down came the second wall.

Yet, there is the **third wall**. The pope believed in self-security. He claimed that he was not subject to temporal powers, but that he was subject to the Scriptures only, with his own interpretation. Now, the third wall was that he held a council illegal unless it was called, or confirmed, by himself. So he was beyond the reach of king or emperor; he was beyond the reach of the Bible; he was beyond the reach of a council. There is a scripture in Matthew 18:15–17, which says: "Moreover, if thy brother shall trespass against thee, go and tell him his fault between thee and him alone; if he shall hear thee, thou hast gained thy brother. But if he will not hear thee, then take with thee one or two more, ... if he shall neglect to hear them, tell it unto the church: but if he neglect to hear the church, let him be unto thee as a heathen man and a publican." Luther, in commenting on this text, said:

> Here, every member is commanded to care for every other. How much rather should we do this when the member that does evil is a ruling member, and by his evil-doing is the cause of much harm and offense to the rest! But if I am to accuse him before the Church, I must bring the Church together.

Note here, Luther claimed that the humblest member of the church had a right to call a council to consider the deeds of a member who had committed offense. Imagine how the pope would consider such a wide departure from the papal idea!

After Luther had smashed the three hypocritical walls that, for four hundred years and more, had been built up around popery and had discussed a number of abuses that Rome had for generations perpetrated on the German people, he then proceeded to mention twenty-seven reforms that should be carried out. Some of these proposed reforms were so radical and so startling that I must here mention a few of them.

1. **Proposal Number One**—The German people should refuse to pay annates to the pope. By the term "annates," were meant a certain form of ecclesiastical taxation, whereby the pope exacted certain gifts from his subjects; which gifts he used to satisfy his own appetite for worldly pleasure. Luther accused the papists of bold robbery and demanded that the German people no longer tolerate the system.

2. **Proposal Number Four**—Luther demanded that no matter of dispute of a temporal nature should be taken to Rome, but that all such cases should be left to the temporal authorities. He agreed that matters of spiritual concern may be properly laid before the pope, but he claimed that it was unscriptural for his Holiness to meddle in temporal affairs. Those things that concern money, property, life, and honor must be settled by temporal judges.

3. **Proposal Number Seven**—It was suggested, in Luther's seventh proposal for reform, that the pope and his court should live in less luxury. Popes in those days lived like kings, only on a grander scale. Luther demanded that the "swarm of vermin at Rome" be diminished in number. This pompous and extravagant living by the pope and his thousands of subordinates, meant a tremendous financial drain on the common people. Luther said that the pope's pomp should be paid by the pope's purse. He pointed out the contrast between the grand living of the

pope, and the humble living of Christ, of whom he professed to be vicar, and the apostle Peter, of whom he claimed to be successor.

4. **Proposal Number Nine**—The pope should have no authority over the emperor, except that he anoints and crowns him at the altar, just as a bishop anoints and crowns a king; and we should not henceforth yield to the devilish pride which compels the emperor to kiss the pope's feet or sit at his feet or, as they claim, hold his stirrup or the bridle of his mule when he mounts for a ride; still less should he do homage and swear faithful allegiance to the pope, as the popes have shamelessly ventured to demand as if they possessed that right.

5. **Proposal Number Eleven**—Luther thought it was silly and blasphemous for people to kiss the pope's feet, so he proposed that they stop the practice. He said it was an unchristian and even anti-Christian thing for a pope, who was nothing but a sinful man, to allow his feet to be kissed by a man who was no worse a sinner than himself. Luther compared Christ and the pope. Christ washed the disciples' feet, and wiped them with a towel, symbolizing the fact that he was their humble servant; and now here comes the pope vaunting himself as the vicar of Christ, and demanding that his subjects pay him the homage of kissing his feet. Luther could not see how "a poor stinking sinner," as he called the pope, could be worthy of such honor.

6. **Proposal Number Twelve**—Pilgrimages to Rome should be abolished, or should be made with the

consent of the town authorities. Luther held that the money spent on such pilgrimages could be more profitably used in caring for the pilgrim's family. It had frequently happened that pious and silly persons had made the journey to the Holy City, leaving their families to exist on the charity of the community at home. Such persons, even though they kissed the pope's feet times unnumbered, were, according to Luther's view, worse than infidels.

7. **Proposal Number Fourteen**—The laws of the Romish Church forbade the marriage of her priests. As a result of this godless demand, many priests lived in open and awful adultery. Luther observed that there was many a pious priest who had been overtaken in immorality, because he had vowed to the Church that he would not marry. Luther knew all this ungodly program concerning the sacred institution of matrimony to be against both divine and natural law, and he demanded that it be abolished.

In closing his Address to the Nobility, Luther said:

> I think too that I have pitched my song in the high key, have made many propositions which will be thought impossible and have attacked many things too sharply. But what am I to do? I am in duty bound to speak.... I know another little song about Rome.... Understandest thou, dear Rome, what I mean? ... Amen.

By the "other little song" that Luther referred to, he meant his booklet on the Babylonian Captivity, in which he assailed the whole Romish system of sacraments. Later, he wrote his Treatise on Christian Liberty. Luther had now broken the last cord that bound him to the Romish Church. He had assailed her doctrines, ridiculed her practices, and defied her authority. He had done the very things for which she had burned more than one person at the stake. Would she also burn Luther? We shall see.

The Burning of the Papal Bull

Chapter 7

Luther Burns Leo's Bull

Luther wrote and Leo raged, but Luther refused to be afraid. He said that truth was more important than his life, and if he perished at the hand of Rome, the truth which he preached would live just the same. It will be remembered that Professor Eck debated with Luther and Carlstadt, and apparently, he won the victory. He felt that he should go to Rome to tell about this victory. And to Rome he went. When he got there, of course, Pope Leo X wanted to know how Luther, the "beast of Wittenberg," was doing. And Eck reported that Luther was growing meaner as he grew older. Leo received the professor with great courtesy, and fatherly consideration. After Eck had bowed and kissed his feet, Leo surprised everybody present by kissing Eck.

Eck stayed around Rome for a while, then returned to Germany. When he went back, he went with a joyous heart, because he carried with him a bull against Luther issued by the Pope. In fact, Eck himself had assisted in drawing up the document, and on June 15, 1520, the Pope signed it. Here is a quotation from it:

Arise, O Lord, arise, judge thy cause, be mindful of the reproaches with which the foolish reproach thee daily. Incline thine ears to our prayers, since foxes have arisen seeking to spoil thy vineyard—whose care, government, and administration thou didst intrust of Peter as its head and thy vicar, and to his successors; the boar out of the woods is seeking to waste it, and a peculiar wild beast does devour it. Arise, O Peter, attend to the cause of the holy Roman Church, mother of all churches, and queen of the church universal arise."

In the bull were then quoted forty-two propositions from Luther's writings. They were taken out of their regular place, and were given a meaning that Luther in no wise intended they should convey. It then continued,

No one of sound mind is ignorant how poisonous, how pernicious, how seductive to godly and simple minds, and finally how contrary to all love and reverence for the holy Roman Church—the foundation and source of all virtue, without which everyone is proved to be an infidel—these errors are.

This bull contained several things of importance. First, it commanded Luther to repent of all he had said and done against the Roman Church. He was to do this by letter if he chose, but the Pope preferred that he should come to Rome in person, in order that there be no doubt as to the genuineness of his submission. Secondly, the bull provided that Luther must quit preaching, teaching, and writing. Certainly, Luther would not do that. His lips insisted on speaking out the message that glowed in his heart. With Paul he could say, "Woe is me if I preach not the gospel." Thirdly, the Pope's bull demanded, not only that he cease to write, but that all his written works must be hunted and burned to ashes. What? Burn all those precious books which defended the liberty of the people's conscience! However, the Pope went still further in this communication. He pronounced all men who sided with Luther as heretics and under the ban of excommunication. These heretics were to be seized whenever possible and sent to Rome! So, it may be seen at once that such a bull issued by the Church was no trivial affair.

For years and years, Rome had not failed to back up such demands, even with death itself. All those who were loyal to the Romish Church rejoiced that at last the famous document had been signed, for they were sure that it would bring about the end of the troublesome Saxon monk. And Luther's friends were sore afraid. They saw with alarm the dark clouds that were gathering thicker and darker over Luther's head, and they feared for the life of the brave defender of the truth. Luther, too, knew he was in great danger, but he trusted God to sustain him as he stood immovable as Gibraltar.

It must not be imagined that this famous bull passed through the Roman political and ecclesiastical machinery in a day. On the contrary it was many weeks, and even months, in the process of preparation. Pope Leo was a man who had given himself over to carnal pleasures. He was more interested in the theater, the chase, and music than he was in the promotion of Biblical Christianity. Sensible men everywhere saw this plainly. There were thousands of people who were with Luther in his views. Even in Rome, there were critics of Rome. There were those who knew there was more fact than fiction in what Luther had been saying about "dear Rome." These persons contended that Luther should be dealt with in moderation. Said they, "Perhaps the German monk, if dealt with reasonably, can be saved to the church: we should take more time for reflection." So the Pope and his advisers were undecided.

But now Dr. Eck came forward in all his fury. He mustered all his forces. The fanatical priests sided with him and gave him new courage. He said that the people in Rome could not know the real danger of the "beast of Wittenberg," as they were such a distance from him. Luther said, "Eck is stirring up the bottomless pit against me." Just at this time, a wealthy banker came to the aid of Eck. He urged the Pope to use every means possible to silence Luther and promised money to aid him in his task. The papacy, always ready to receive money, was glad for the generous offer. The decision was made. Luther was condemned, if he did not retract in sixty days, and Eck was happy.

When the bull against Luther had been duly drawn up and signed, a question arose: Who should be the messenger to carry it to Germany? There were several persons around Rome who were anxious to have this distinction. In Eck's conceited mind, he himself was the proper person to carry the bull to Germany. Why should he not be? He had been the bitter enemy of Luther for years. He had disputed with him at Leipzig. He was fully aware of all the dangers to the church that existed in Germany. He was conceited enough, flattering enough, impudent enough, and drunken enough, to do an excellent job in carrying this project to a successful end. So against the will of many sensible men, even in Rome, he was appointed special nuncio[†] to convey

---

† A *nuncio* is a permanent diplomatic representative of the pope at a foreign court or capital.

the document to Germany. Imagine his joy and exaltation as he left the city of the seven hills with victory itself in his hands. He had Luther's condemnation right with him. Victory! Victory! Victory! was his watchword as he crossed the Alps and made his way into Germany.

Nonetheless, was not God on his throne? Eck's pride was soon changed to humiliation. He had expected to be received in Germany with great enthusiasm. However, many people were indifferent toward the professor and his message, and more were decidedly hostile. He had hoped to have the bull published far and wide in Germany, but the bishops refused to give it publicity. If posted at all in certain towns, it was put in places where it was not generally read. Even the protector, Duke George, was not favorable to its publication. When full of wine, Eck displayed the bull and boasted how he "intended bringing that scoundrel, Martin, to reason." He took lodging at Leipzig, where he suffered much humiliation. A group of students posted up placards in a number of places, condemning and ridiculing Dr. Eck. Things became so warm for him, that he fled into a cloister, where Tetzel had formerly been in hiding, and there he refused to be interviewed. The students composed a sarcastic song about him and sang where he could hear it. Eck was much cast down. A throng of students came from Luther's university and raged out against him. One night, Eck slipped out of his hiding place and left the city. Some students at Erfurt, when copies of the bull were posted at their university, tore them down, and threw them in the river, exclaiming, "Since it is a bull [a bubble], let it float."

Eck frequently got drunk, but he always remained sober enough to stay away from Wittenberg in person.

So he sent his bull there and demanded that it be published. Was it published? "I know nothing of Eck," said Luther, "except that he has arrived [from Rome] with a long beard, a long bull, and a long purse; but I laugh at his bull.... I despise and attack it as impious, false, and in every respect worthy of Eck. It is Christ Himself who is condemned therein. No reasons are given in it. I am cited to Rome, not to be heard, but that I may eat my words. Oh, that Charles V would act like a man; and that for the love of Christ he would attack these wicked spirits. I rejoice in having to bear such ills for the best of causes. Already I feel greater liberty in my heart." Luther wrote a tract about this time entitled, The New Bull and the Lies of Eck.

The Pope caused many of Luther's writings to be burned; Luther paid him back in his own change. When Eck sent the bull to Wittenberg, the professors refused to post it but, instead, posted this notice in a public place on Monday, December 10:

> All friends are invited to assemble about nine o'clock at the church of the Holy Cross outside the city walls, where the godless books of the papal constitutions and scholastic theology will be burned according to ancient and apostolic usage, inasmuch as the boldness of the enemies of the gospel has waxed so great that they have cast the godly, evangelical books of Dr. Luther into the fire. Come pious and zealous youth, to this pious and religious spectacle, for it is now the time when the antichrist must be exposed.

When nine o'clock came, a great crowd of students and professors had gathered about the university buildings. Luther himself headed the procession. They marched outside of the town and built a bonfire. When the flames were blazing in the air, and the smoke was curling toward the sky, Luther stepped forward with the Pope's bull in his hand. Imagine, if you can, the serious look on everyone's face when he threw the bull into the flames, as he uttered these words, "Because thou hast brought down the truth of God, he also brings thee down unto this fire today. Amen." Luther returned quietly to his room, where he wrote a tract explaining why he had burned the Pope's bull. A number of students celebrated the occasion by singing songs ridiculing the Pope. They obtained a wagon, went from house to house through the city, and, collecting all the Catholic books they could find, piled them on the fire. Near the place where the fire was built is an oak tree known as Luther's Oak. Every year it is visited by hundreds of tourists, who read this inscription on a tablet, "Dr. Martin Luther burned, at this place, on December 10, 1520, the papal bull."

The next day, after Dr. Luther had burned the bull, he lectured in the assembly room of the university to a vast audience of students and doctors. He condemned the papacy in the hottest terms and called upon all who were present to stand solidly for reformation. His address produced a profound effect on the students. They

Dr. Luther

regarded Luther as a messenger sent by God to declare the truth, as indeed he was.

It will be remembered that the bull was dated June 15, and that it gave Luther sixty days to humble himself, and apologize to the Pope. It was nearly Christmas when Luther burned the bull. He had become more bold with the passing months. It was now very plain to Pope Leo X that Luther did not intend to revoke his theses. On January 3, 1521, he issued a final bull of excommunication in which Luther and those who followed him were cut off from the Church and consigned to the punishment that the Church provided for heretics. So we see Luther as an outlaw under the curse of the Roman Church, the most humanly powerful religious force then on earth. What will he do? What will become of him? Will God forsake him? We shall see.

The Pope

A Roman Catholic Bishop

Chapter 8

Luther Before the Emperor

Germany's new emperor was just a boy—Charles V, who was only about twenty years of age. After a hot political fight, he had succeeded in getting himself elected as head of the Holy Roman Empire which included the German nation. However, Charles V knew and cared little about things German. He was not in sympathy with German traditions, nor German sentiment. He did not even understand the German language. There was one thing that Charles was anxious to do, and that was to keep the favor of Pope Leo X. Though he was young, he was wise enough to know that Pope Leo could have a large influence in helping him to realize any of his political ambitions.

So far as Martin Luther was concerned, Charles cared nothing for him any more than to use him, if possible, as a tool to further his own interests with the Pope. However, Frederick, Elector of Saxony, was a friend to Luther, and he had great power with Charles V. It was largely through Frederick's influence that Charles was exalted to the throne. Frederick had been offered the crown himself, but was too wise to accept it under the existing circumstances. If it had not been for Frederick, Charles would have made things much more unpleasant for Luther than he did.

On November 17, Luther had made an appeal from the pope to a general church council, composed of the dignitaries of the church.

In January, 1521, Charles V, a few months after the day on which he was crowned, opened his first assembly of the Empire, or diet, at Worms, an old and historic city up the Rhine River. It was before this council that Luther was to stand and defend, or revoke, the books he had written against the Romish system. Pope Leo X sent to this council, as his representative, one Aleander, who is represented as a shrewd and courteous liar. He was a smooth politician and left no stones unturned to see that Luther received the worst that Rome could give. An imperial edict was issued, upon an order from Pope Leo to Charles V that the bull of ex-communication against Luther should be carried out in Germany. On it, Aleander made a speech three hours long before the diet. In eloquent terms, he pleaded with the council that Luther's writings were sufficient to justify the burning of the Wittenberg monk. He insisted that Luther should not be permitted to come before the diet. He had already been condemned by the great head of the Church, the pope; and was not that sufficient? Why waste the time of the Emperor, and princes, in listening to the babblings of a contemptible monk? But his eloquence did not win the day, and after much debate, it was decided that Luther himself should be called before the council.

It was late in March, 1521, when a messenger sent from Charles reached Luther, and informed him that he was to come before the council to furnish information concerning the books and papers he had been writing. When the messenger, accompanied by a servant reached the town of Wittenberg, he found Luther in poor health; quietly at work in the University. This is the message that was carried to Luther:

Charles, by the grace of God Emperor elect of the Romans, ...

Honorable, well-beloved, and pious—We and the states of the holy empire here assembled, having resolved to institute an inquiry touching the doctrine and the books that thou hast lately published, have issued, for thy coming hither, and thy return to a place of security, our safe-conduct and that of the empire, which we send thee herewith. Our sincere desire is, that thou shouldst prepare immediately for this journey, in order that within the space of twenty-one days fixed by our safe-conduct, thou mayest without fail be present before us. Fear neither injustice nor violence. We will firmly abide by our aforesaid safe-conduct, and expect that thou will comply with our summons. In so doing, thou wilt obey our earnest wishes.

Given in our imperial city of Worms, the sixth day of March,

in the year of our Lord, 1521, and the second of our reign.

—Charles

Would Luther go to Worms? And what would happen to him if he went? Would the Emperor's promise of safety be kept? Had not Huss been given just such a promise of safety, when he went to the Council of Constance, and had he not been killed in spite of such a safe-conduct? What would Luther do? What would most men do in his place?

His friends were alarmed. All over Germany there was a great stir. Those who believed in the Reformation were uneasy, fearing lest the reformer, in going to Worms, was going to his death. The Elector, Frederick, Luther's great protector, expressed grave fears.

As for Luther himself, he saw the danger, but he did not fear it. He believed that God would shield him if it were His will, and if it were not His will he did not care to be shielded. We hear him at this time saying,

> Fear not that I shall retract a single syllable.... If the Emperor summons me that I may be put to death as an enemy of the empire, I am ready to comply with his call; for with the help of Christ, I will never desert the word on the battlefield. I am well aware that these blood-thirsty men will never rest until they have taken away my life.

When Elector Frederick had asked him if he were willing to come to Worms if called, he had replied,

> If I am called, I shall go; and if I were too sick to go, I shall have them carry me. It was wrong to doubt that God calls me when the emperor calls.

On seeing the concern of his friends for his welfare, Luther said:

> The papists do not desire my coming to Worms, but my condemnation and my death. It matters not. Pray not for me, but for the word of God. Before my blood has grown cold, thousands of men in the whole world will have become responsible for having shed it. The most holy adversary of Christ, the father, the master, the generalissimo of murderers, insists on its being shed. So be it. Let God's will be done. Christ will give me his Spirit to overcome these ministers of error. I despise them during my life; I shall triumph over them during my life; I shall triumph over them by my death.

So amidst the tears of his friends, on April 2, Luther left his beloved Wittenberg for Worms. Would he ever return? It was doubtful, very doubtful. He turned to Melanchthon, his great partner in the work, and said with a trembling voice, "My dear brother, if I do not return, and my enemies put me to death, continue to teach and stand fast in the truth. Labor in my stead, since I shall no longer be able to labor for myself. If you survive, my death will be of little consequence." Then, with three companions, he climbed into a common canvas-covered wagon, furnished by the town, and began his journey to Worms. The distance from Wittenberg to Worms was something near three hundred miles, according to the route of travel. Luther had to pass through many towns and cities before reaching

there. Everybody along the way was eager to see the man who was bold enough to oppose the religious and civil leaders of Europe. They had heard of him, and now they must see him with their own eyes. In every town his path was thronged with people. Many of them hailed him as a great hero. Others insulted him as a despised nuisance. His friends feared he would be killed at Worms, and his enemies feared he would not. But in spite of friends or enemies, he would go. He said he would go if the devils in Worms were as thick as the tiles on the roofs of the houses.

When he reached the town of Naumburg, he met a certain priest. This priest had a picture of Savonarola, who had been condemned to death in Italy by Pope Alexander VI, and was burned for trying to do the very same thing Luther was trying to do—reform the Church. This priest was a friend of Luther's work, and he meant this act as a silent warning to him of what the Church did to those who opposed her. However, it would take more than the pictures of martyrs to scare this bold German monk. So he continued on his journey. When he drew near the city of Erfurt, where he had attended school, and had sung for something to eat, in the gloomy days of his youth, he was met by a large group of horsemen who had come out to welcome him. These were leading men of the city and University at Erfurt, and they had made arrangements for Luther to speak to a great crowd of people at a church while there. When they left Erfurt, he and his three traveling companions were joined by three or four persons who journeyed on with them to Worms. One of these new companions was a young lawyer by the name of Justus

Jonas who, from that time on, came to be a close friend and helper of Luther in the work of the Reformation.

As the days and hours brought Luther and his company nearer and nearer Worms, all was excitement. The news of their coming went before them. His enemies would have made away with him but for the King's safe-conduct. Luther sent word to a friend of his, who was at Worms, to prepare lodging for him. On the morning of April 16, Luther's wagon drew in sight of the walls of the city. It was at the noon hour when the wagon passed through its gates. The day, the hour, the moment, had actually arrived when the famous monk was in the city. The city went wild with excitement. The citizens were sitting at their noon meal when Luther entered. Leaving their table, they rushed into the streets, to get a glimpse of him whom the Pope sought to kill. The streets were so crowded that with difficulty Luther made his way to the hotel, in which he was to find lodging. When he stepped from his wagon to the ground, he uttered these words, "God will be my defense," and God was.

When the Emperor, Charles V, heard that Luther had arrived, he was much agitated. He said, "Luther is come, what must we do?" Luther spent the afternoon and evening at his hotel resting. He also received visitors, who thronged the place by the scores, eager to see him. Charles V called the council to meet at four o'clock the next afternoon, and Luther was notified to that effect on the morning of that eventful day.

When the clock struck the hour of four, on the afternoon of April 17, 1521, all the people waited breathlessly to see what that hour would bring forth. Martin Luther trembled, as he recognized that he was being brought before the greatest tribunal in the world. However, he was brave, and he followed the marshal and the herald, who were sent to bring him into the hall. The herald went first, the marshal next, and Luther came last. But the streets were so crowded that they could not get through, and they were obliged to enter the doors of private houses, and go through back yards and gardens to the place where the council was sitting. When they reached the door of the town hall, they could not get in for the people. "Make way, make way," they shouted, but no one moved. By force, the soldiers cleared a way, and they pushed through the crowd into the building.

And there the son of the poor miner stood before a court as great, if not greater, as that before which a man had ever stood. This council was made up of the mighty ones of the earth—emperor, kings, barons, dukes, princes, nobles, electors, bishops, prelates, and ambassadors—in all, two hundred and four persons. As Luther stood before the dazzling throne of Charles V, all eyes were turned on him. For a time he seemed overcome with the splendor of the surroundings, and was unable to speak. For a moment terrible and awful silence reigned. An officer rose and broke the silence with these words, which he spoke first in Latin, and then in German: "Martin Luther, his sacred and invincible imperial majesty has cited you before his throne, in accordance with the advice and counsel of the states of the Holy Roman Empire, to require you to answer two questions: First, do you acknowledge these books [on the table] to have been written by you? Second, are you prepared to retract these books and their contents; or do you persist in the opinions you have advanced in them?"

Luther acknowledged that he had written the books. However, the second question, "Will you retract them, or apologize for them?" he did not want to answer

Luther before Charles V

without time to think it over. The emperor, and his counselors, agreed to give Luther twenty-four hours, in which to decide how he would answer that second question, "Will you retract?" Luther went back to his hotel, and spent most of the night in prayer.

It was a terrible night for him. It seemed at times that God had forsaken him. He prayed again and again. Finally, he reached the place where his heart said, "Amen," to God's will, and his mind was at peace. At four o'clock in the afternoon of April 18, he was again taken to the hall where the council was sitting. The great crowd packed the hall and court making the atmosphere warm and sultry. Luther was obliged to remain outside in the court for two hours or more, while the council was engaged in other matters. Here he was gazed upon by the surging mass of friends and enemies, all anxious to lay eyes upon the famous monk.

At last, when it had grown dark, and the candles were lighted, Luther was again brought before the council, where he was again asked to answer the second question put to him the day before; namely, "Will you retract the books you have written?" Luther addressed the Emperor and the princes in the German language, using the most humble terms. He made a rather long address in which he apologized for some strong terms he had used against his enemies, which terms he granted were unwise. As for retracting any of the doctrines put forth in his books, he utterly refused, unless he was first convinced that they were not in accordance with the Scripture. In case his books were proved to be unscriptural, he said that he would be the first to throw them in the fire.

When Luther had finished his address in German, he was nearly worn out; but he was required to give it also in Latin, as the Emperor did not understand German. It seemed impossible for him to go on with it, but the Lord helped him, and he repeated it in Latin, with great vigor. The orator for the council was much amazed at Luther's speech and demanded that he answer the question, "yes," or "no." To this Luther replied, "Since your most serene majesty and your high mightiness require from me a clear, simple, and precise answer I will give you one.... I cannot, and I will not retract.... Here I stand; I can do no other; may God help me! Amen!" Amid great confusion, Luther was taken back to his hotel.

Wartburg Castle

Chapter 9

Kidnapped by Friends

It was on Thursday, April 18, 1521, that Luther took his noble stand before the Emperor and the representatives of the Pope. The whole city of Worms was in turmoil. Everybody was excited. Many were against Luther. Many were for him. Some praised him. Others denounced him. Through it all, the great reformer remained calm and unshaken. His hotel was thronged by the multitude of persons who sought to speak with him. He was busy night and day talking with friends of the Reformation, and making plans for carrying on the great work which he had begun. As to himself, he knew little of what might happen to him; but in any event, his work must be carried on. His safe-conduct was about to expire, but, at the command of the Emperor, on April 26, he mounted his wagon and started back to Wittenberg. In the wagon with him were his brother, James Luther, and two other persons. "The villain is gone. We shall do our best," said Aleander, the Pope's man; meaning, of course, that he and his helpers would do their best to see that Luther was put to death.

It has been stated before that this Aleander was a shrewd and courteous liar, and it is not at all surprising that Charles should have him write up the edict which was to declare the monk an outlaw. This edict was a fierce and terrible piece of writing. It declared that Luther was a beastly outlaw, and that he should be captured, dead or alive, and brought before the authorities. His writings were to be burned, and his property and that of his followers was not to be respected. This edict was written by Aleander, and on the morning of May 26, just after mass in the church, it was signed by the Emperor.

Meanwhile Luther was on his way back to Wittenberg. He stopped on his way to visit his feeble old grandmother, who died soon afterward. After receiving the blessings of his grandmother, Luther resumed his journey to Wittenberg. As the wagon drew near the Castle of Altenstein, in the Thuringian Mountains, it passed through a small ravine, in following the winding road that skirted the dense woods. It was near the close of the day, and darkness was beginning to settle over the thick forest. All of a sudden a noise was heard, and there came rushing out of the dark forest, five masked men on horses. They were armed from head to foot. When James Luther saw them, he sprang from the wagon, and escaped into the woods. One of the masked men held the driver, while another one of them engaged Amsdorf, the third member of the party in the wagon. The other three masked men seized Luther bodily, set him on a horse that they led, and made their escape with him among the trees. They wandered up and down in the woods, retracing their steps now and then, in order that their trail might not be followed.

Luther, unused to horseback riding, was overcome with fatigue and was compelled to stop and rest a while near a beech tree, where he drank from a spring that still bears his name.

When Luther had rested a short while, they again mounted their horses and continued wandering around through the forest until nearly midnight, when they came to the foot of a mountain. At the top of this hill was an old castle, which had been occupied for generations by German nobles and princes. The name of the castle was the Wartburg, and the hill on the top of which it stood was near the town of Eisenach. When the five masked men who had captured Luther came to the foot of this hill, they turned their horses' heads towards the castle at its top. They put Luther in this castle and locked him up. The people in it did not know who the newcomer was. They were told by the lord of the castle that his name was Knight George, and he was known by that name during his entire stay there. He was dressed in the clothes of a knight, that is, a soldier of a certain rank. He was also told to let his beard grow, which he did.

The persons who were in the wagon with Luther when he was captured drove on to Wittenberg. All along the way, they spread the news of what had happened to the great Luther. He was gone. Where he was taken, and who had taken him there, they could not say. They only knew that five burly men with great swords and mysterious masks had carried him away. All Germany was excited. The friends of the Pope and Emperor rejoiced. The friends of Luther and the Reformation mourned. Some were sure that his dead body had been found in an old mine; and still others thought that he had escaped into Denmark, where he was sheltered by the king of that country.

I shall now tell how it was planned to capture Luther and carry him away to the castle. It will be remembered that Frederick was Elector of Saxony, and that he was a staunch friend of Luther and his cause. Frederick knew very well of the political and religious tricks of Rome and her representatives. He was always uneasy for the welfare of the reformer. When he saw the bold stand which Luther took at Worms, he knew the great danger into which the reformer was thrown. He must plan for the safety of the monk. So before Luther left Worms, Frederick sent certain persons to Wittenberg. They did not let Luther know, however, of this plan to capture him lest he should object. Their plans were all laid and when Luther and his party reached a certain point in the road, they sprang upon him. Their plans were so well carried out that even Frederick did not at first, know just where Luther was in hiding. It was well that he did not, for when Charles V asked him where Luther was, he could truthfully say that he did not know.

While Luther was confined in Wartburg Castle, he often grew weary of a life so different from the exciting and active life of a few months before. From his lonely room he could look out over the dark, gloomy forest that surrounded the castle. When he looked into the mirror, he scarcely knew himself, with his military clothes and long and shaggy beard and hair. The fine food, which was furnished him, and the lack of exercise weakened his health. In back of the castle, on the hill beside the paths, grew an abundance of strawberries. Luther was sometimes allowed to go outside the castle

Who is Really Your God?

An Excerpt From Martin Luther's LARGE CATECHISM[†]

The First Commandment:

> You must not have other gods.
>
> That is, I must be your only God.

Question: What does this saying mean? How should we understand it? What does it mean to have a god? What is God?

Answer: To have a god means this: You expect to receive all good things from it and turn to it in every time of trouble. Yes, to have a god means to trust and to believe in Him with your whole heart. I have often said that only the trust and faith of the heart can make a god or an idol. If your faith and trust are true, you have the true God, too. On the other hand, where trust is false, is evil; there you will not have the true God either. Faith and God live together. I tell you, whatever you set your heart on and rely on is really your god.

[†] This text was translated from the German *Triglot Concordia* (p. 580) for the Project Wittenberg by Rev. Robert E. Smith and is in the public domain.

gate and stroll through the woods to gather these berries. He was always attended by a guard, however. In this way, Luther wandered farther and farther away from the castle in his military garb. One day, he and his guard were on one of these rounds when they stopped at a monastery where Luther had stayed all night a few months before, on his way to Worms. As Luther was wandering around the place, one of the attendants recognized him. The guard, seeing the dangerous situation, prevailed on Luther to hasten away, and they were well on their way back to the castle before the fellow at the monastery recovered from his amazement.

The ten months which the reformer spent at the Wartburg were not a period of luxurious idleness. The little room, with its old-fashioned bed, chair, table, and wooden chest, was the scene of much labor. His pen was always busy, and a powerful pen it was. He wrote dozens and even hundreds of letters, tracts, papers, and books during his confinement. When he was first captured by the masked horsemen, many of the Catholics thought he was dead; but when the stream of writings began to pour forth from his pen they discovered, to their sorrow, that Luther was still very much alive. The greatest work that he did, while in the castle, was the translation of the New Testament into the German language. He based his movement upon the idea that every man should read and understand the Bible for himself. If they were to read the blessed Book, understand it, and put it into practice in their lives, they must have it translated into their own language. Luther had in his possession no dictionaries, no concordance, and no reference books. He probably had only his Greek and Latin copy, but he had a will to work and when he left the castle in March, 1522, the translation of the New Testament was complete. The first copies were printed at Wittenberg about seven months later, and the German people scrambled to get them, in order that they might read for themselves the blessed Word of Life. Luther's German Bible, to this day, is recognized as a wonderful piece of German literature.

Cover Plate of Luther's German Bible

Philip Melanchthon, Luther's Friend

Chapter 10

Back at Wittenberg

While Luther was quiet in his room in Wartburg Castle, there was no quietness in his home town, Wittenberg. The city had filled up with religious extremists. From all over Germany and from many other countries in Europe, these rowdy fools came pouring into Wittenberg. These people were doing all sorts of silly things in the name of religion. Dr. Carlstadt lost all reason. He told the students at the University to go home and quit studying, because God was pleased to show men the truth without their studying. He put on plain workman's clothes and was often seen going with his Bible under his arm to the most ignorant man in the whole town to have the Scriptures explained. These fanatics went into the Catholic churches, broke in pieces the images, and tore up the church furniture. They ridiculed all those who did not believe as they did. They brought great reproach on the cause of the Reformation, for the Catholics accused them of belonging to the reform party, and poor Luther was blamed for stirring up all this trouble.

All this news reached Luther's ears at the castle on the hill. When he heard it, he was grieved. He spent sleepless nights. He knew that the cause of God was suffering. But who could stop all these crazy doings at Wittenberg? The Catholics could not; the doctors and professors at Wittenberg were powerless. In fact, many of them had gone over fully to the side of the fanatics. Even Melanchthon was alarmed and knew not what to do. The wise and good elector, Frederick, was puzzled. If only Luther were there! And Luther wanted very much to be there; but if he left his hiding-place in the castle, the Pope and the Emperor would surely kill him for he was still under the ban. The Elector would not agree for him to leave the castle. What would Luther do? He had already, in November of the previous year, stolen out of the castle, made a flying trip to Wittenberg, and returned. He wrote his friends at Wittenberg to look out for him, for he was coming again. On March 3, he stepped from behind the Wartburg walls. He said good-bye to the quiet old place and went down the hill and out into the world. In going from behind the sheltering wall of Wartburg, into the world, he knew that he might be going to his death, but he felt that it was the call of duty; so he did not falter.

Once outside the walls he began the five days' journey to Wittenberg. When he was near the city of Jena, he was overtaken by a thunderstorm. He stopped at Black Bear hotel. He was still dressed in his soldier's garb; and, of course, no one even guessed that it was Luther. While he was sitting by a table reading, two young men from Switzerland, their boots and clothing drenched with mud and rain, entered the room and sat near the door. Luther soon struck up a conversation with the young men, and they told him that they were on their way to Wittenberg to attend the university there. They said that they had heard so much of Martin Luther that they were determined to see him, and they wanted to know if the stranger could tell whether or not Luther was at Wittenberg. The stranger answered that he knew Luther was not there, but that he soon would be there. The young men were greatly joyed at the prospect of seeing the famous monk. The stranger asked them how Luther was regarded in Switzerland. They replied that some almost worshiped him, and others thought he was a contemptible servant of Satan. When they had finished supper the stranger shook hands with the two young men and said, "When you get to Wittenberg, remember me to Jerome Schurff." "Whom shall we remember, sir?" replied one of the young men. "Say only that he that will soon come sends his greetings," said the stranger.

A few days later, the young men reached Wittenberg and called to see Dr. Schurff and Philip Melanchthon, possibly to bear them the message from the stranger. But who should they see in the room but that same stranger. And here they found the "stranger" was Luther himself.

Luther was not unconscious of the danger of his position in traveling over the country when the Emperor had given orders that he was to be captured by whomsoever should meet him. But he had felt that he simply could not stay at the Wartburg any longer, when there was such need of him at Wittenberg. On his way from the castle to Wittenberg, he stopped at the small town of Borna long enough to write a letter to the Elector Frederick, his great friend and protector. Here is what he says:

Grace and peace from God our Father, and from our Lord Jesus Christ.

Most Serene Elector, Gracious Lord.

The events that have taken place at Wittenberg, to the great reproach of the gospel, have caused me such pain, that if I were not confident of the truth of our cause, I should have given way to despair...I have sufficiently given way to your highness by passing this year in retirement. The devil knows well that I did so not through fear. I should have entered Worms had there been as many devils in the city as tiles on the housetops. Now, Duke George[†] with whom your highness frightens me, is much less to be feared than a single devil. If that which is passing at Wittenberg were taking place at Leipzig [the Duke's residence], I would immediately mount my horse to go thither, although ... for nine whole days together it were to rain nothing but Duke Georges, and each one nine times more furious than he is. What does he think of in attacking me? Does he take Christ my Lord for a man of straw?

Luther goes on in this letter to explain to the Elector that he is trusting in God to protect him. He appreciates what the Elector has done for him and is willing to do, but he tells him that human hands are too feeble to protect in such a time as this; so he prefers to leave all in the hands of God. In closing the letter, he says,

I have written this letter in haste, that you may not be made uneasy at hearing of my arrival. I have to do with a very different man from Duke George. He knows me well, and I know him pretty well. Given at Borna, at the inn of the Guide, this Ash Wednesday, 1522.

Your electoral highness
Very humble servant, Martin Luther.

---

†   Duke George was a bitter enemy of Luther, who had to pass through the duke's territory to reach Wittenberg.

When Luther entered the town of Wittenberg on March 6, 1522, after having spent five days on the road, it was a day of profound joy. It was like the homecoming of a father. Students, teachers, citizens, doctors, entered into the rejoicings. The following Sunday, Luther stood in the pulpit of the Wittenberg church. His coming had been noised over the city. "Luther has come! Luther has come!" was on everyone's lips. The church was crowded to the doors with those who were eager to hear the hero of Worms. They breathlessly listened when he stood up to speak. He spoke, that morning, with great boldness and humility. He preached from the text, "All things are lawful unto me, but all things are not expedient." He admonished the people for the rough way in which they had been handling things and told them that their fanatical actions were bringing reproach on the whole Reformation. He said, in his second sermon:

> Compel or force anyone with power I will not, for faith must be gentle and unforced. Take an example by me. I opposed indulgences and all the papists, but not with force; I only wrote, preached, and used God's Word, and nothing else. That Word, while I slept, ... has broken the papacy more than any king or emperor ever broke it. Had I wished it, I might have brought Germany to civil war. Yes, at Worms I might have started a game which would not have been safe for the Emperor, but it would have been a fool's game. So I did nothing, but only let the Word act.

Luther preached every day for a solid week, with great fervor and power. These sermons are models of pulpit eloquence. They brought about the desired result. Common sense gained the day. Order, for the time being, was restored, fanaticism was checked, the "prophets" turned to other fields, and once more

Luther was the hero of the great Reformation movement.

Luther Preaching

Chapter 11

Luther in Love

Luther lived in Wittenberg, in the "Black Cloister," formerly the monastery there. It was not made of black stone, but of red brick. It was called the Black Cloister because of the long black robes worn by the group of monks, of which Luther had been one, who had lived there. It was very large, with long rows of cell-like rooms. It must be remembered that the Catholic Church did not allow her priests or monks to marry, and Luther and his fellow monks lived in this cloister for years without a woman there, unless perhaps a maid or two were kept to aid in housework. When Luther received the light of God's Word along other lines, he also obtained it on the subject of ministers' marrying. He began to teach and preach that it was the privilege of a priest to marry if he so desired. This, he said, was a thousand times better than for them to remain single and live in such shameful immorality, as was practiced by a great many of them. Of course, the papists criticized him for this teaching, and called him a lustful beast. But what did Luther care for that? He had braved the storms for so many years, he was growing used to them.

When the reformers began to teach that every man had a right to marry if he so pleased, and that it was not necessary for a lot of monks to be bunched together in a monastery to keep holy, these institutions

Luther's Dove Seal

began to lose their population. Many monks married and entered upon some secular occupation in order to make an honest living for their wives and families. All the monks had left Black Cloister at Wittenberg save two—Luther and one other remained. And it was a lonely life, indeed. The great, gloomy building was a cheerless spot for the brave reformer.

On January 29, 1499—fifteen years after Martin Luther was born—there came into the world, in a little town a few miles south of Leipzig, Germany, a baby girl. Her parents named her Catherine. When she grew older she was commonly called Katie. Her father's name was Hans von Bora. When Katie was still a baby her mother died. A few years later, Katie's father married again, and when Katie was five years old she was sent away from home to a convent school, where her father intended that she should become a nun. In this school, the little girl was shut away from the outside world. Here she spent the quiet days in prayer, teaching, reading, and doing works of charity. In this way she became quite well educated for a girl of those days, and at the age of sixteen she was consecrated a nun. Of course, it was expected that Katie would spend her whole life behind the doors of the convent. Such a life was considered by the Catholic Church as the proper life for any pious woman to lead. However, when the monks, after Luther's preaching, began to leave the monasteries and go out into the free and open world, then the nuns in the nunneries thought they could do likewise; and they did. Of course, to get out of the nunnery was a hard thing to do, and any one who was caught assisting a nun to escape was dealt with severely, as was also any nun who tried to escape. Then, once out of the nunnery, the nuns knew not where to go nor what to do.

On the night of April 4, 1523, three men appeared at the nunnery in the town of Grimma, where Katie, anxious to escape, was kept. The men, one of whom was a rich business man, assisted twelve of the younger nuns to escape. Katie was one of the twelve. Three of these women went to live with their relatives, but nine did not know where to go. Katie was one of the nine. They were finally brought to Wittenberg, where it was hoped that Luther would help them. He wrote a letter concerning them to his friend, George Spalatin:

Wittenberg, April 10, 1523.

Grace and peace. Nine fugitive nuns, a wretched crowd, have been brought to me by honest citizens of Torgau. I mean Leonard Coppe and his nephew, Wolf Tomitzsch; there is therefore no cause for suspicion. I pity them much, but most of all the others who are dying everywhere in such numbers in their cursed and impure celibacy. This sex, so very, very weak, joined by nature or rather by God to the other, perishes when cruelly separated. O tyrants! O cruel parents and kinsmen in Germany!

You ask what I shall do with them? First, I shall inform their relatives and ask them to support the girls; if they will not, I shall have the girls otherwise provided for. Some of the families have already promised me to take them; for some I shall get husbands, if I can. Their names are: Magdalene von Staupitz, Elsa von Canitz, Ave Gross, Ave von Schonfeld and her sister Margaret, Laneta von Goltz, Margaret and Catherine Zeschau and Catherine von Bora. Here are they, who serve Christ, in need of true pity. They have escaped from the cloister in miserable condition. I pray you also do the work of charity and beg some money for me from your rich courtiers, by which I can support the girls a week or two until their kinsmen or others provide for them.... The poor, who would willingly give, have nothing; the rich either refuse or give so reluctantly that they lose the credit of the gift with God and take up my time begging from them. Nothing is too much for the world and its way. Of my annual salary I have only ten or fifteen gulden left, besides which not a penny has been given me by my brothers or by the city. But I ask them for nothing, to emulate the boast of Paul, despoiling other churches to serve my Corinthians free...."

Farewell and pray for me,

Martin Luther.

Luther exercised himself much in finding homes for these nine runaway nuns. One of them found a home in Grimma, and one, through the influence of Luther, secured a position as a teacher. Some of them returned to their relatives, and others married. Three remained in Wittenberg. Katie was one of the three, the other two were Ave Schonfeld and her sister Margaret. Luther, it seems, fell in love with Ave, but for some reason the courtship did not develop into matrimony. Luther had not intended to marry. He said he was neither wood nor stone, and like any normal man had desires toward matrimony, but he saw the clouds of persecution that hung dark above his head, and he expected at any time he might meet the death of the heretic. He was still under the ban of the Pope and the Emperor, and his great friend and protector, Frederick, was dead. He did not wish to marry and leave his wife so soon a widow.

Finally, Ave and Margaret Schonfeld both married and went away from Wittenberg. Only one of the nine runaway nuns was left there. Katie was the one. She was taken into the home of a rich man who had formerly been burgomaster of Wittenberg. Here she lived for two years and became quite an expert in housekeeping and other useful work. By her splendid traits of character, rather than by her beauty, she won the respect and admiration of all who came in contact with her. Because of her goodness, she was even nicknamed "St. Catherine of Siena."

Jerome Baumgartner, a young man who lived at Nuremberg, had attended the University of Wittenberg. He had graduated from there in 1521 and had then returned to his native town. Two years later, he had come back to Wittenberg to visit his old teacher Professor Melanchthon. While in Wittenberg, he won the heart of Katie and went back to his home town with the understanding that he was to return to Wittenberg and wed Katie. He never returned. The reason for his failure to return is not definitely known, but it was a crushing blow to the affectionate heart of the orphan girl. Luther wrote to Jerome in these words, "If you want Katie you had best act quickly before she is given to someone else who wants her. She has not yet conquered her love for you, and I would willingly see you married to each other." Nevertheless, Jerome married a rich girl.

A certain Dr. Glatz sought the hand of Katie. Luther in all good faith undertook to plead the case of Dr. Glatz and urged Katie to marry the doctor. Katie was rather frank and replied that she utterly refused to wed Dr. Glatz, but had no objection to marrying Dr. Luther. This set the reformer to thinking, as might be expected, and he married Katie the following June.

Luther teaches his students around his table.

Chapter 12

Luther at Home

Two weeks after Luther and Katie were married, they celebrated their wedding. This was June 27, 1525. It was a happy event for Luther. Many of his friends in all parts of Germany were invited, and not a few accepted. His aged father and mother were present, and they greatly rejoiced. They had encouraged Luther in his marriage. Luther wrote on June 21 to a friend of the affair and said, "God has suddenly and unexpectedly caught me in the bond of a holy matrimony. I intent to celebrate with a wedding breakfast on Thursday. That my parents and all good friends may be merry, my Lord Catherine and I kindly beg you to send us, at my cost and as quickly as possible, a barrel of the best Torgau beer." It seems strange to us now that as great and good a man as Martin Luther should celebrate his wedding by drinking beer. We must bear in mind, however, that in this time, people thought no more of drinking beer than we think now of drinking cider or lemonade. Men like Luther sincerely believed that if Christ made wine at a wedding, then Christians were at liberty to drink it in moderation. At the celebration, the Luthers received

Luther and His wife, Catherine von Bora

many presents from persons of distinction. The elector remembered them with a gift. Martin and Katie, like most happy "newly-weds," on this occasion sat to have their picture painted.

When Luther married, he created almost as big a sensation as when he had nailed his Ninety-Five Theses to the church door, nearly eight years before this time. The pope accused him of every vile thing imaginable and said he had broken away from the doctrine of priestly celibacy in order that he might gratify his own passions. Most of his friends questioned the advisability of his marriage, and some of them criticized him severely. However, Luther wrote to his friend Amsdorf, "I married to gratify my father, who asked me to marry and leave him descendants.... I was not carried away by passion, for I do not love my wife that way, but esteem her as a friend." To George Spalatin he wrote, "I have made myself so cheap and despised by this marriage that I expect the angels laugh and the devils weep thereat. The world and its wise men have not yet seen how pious and sacred is marriage, but they consider it impious and devilish in me. It pleases me, however, to have my marriage condemned by those who are ignorant of God."

When Katie came to be mistress of the Black Cloister, at the touch of her hands its long halls and gloomy corridors were soon lighted up with the sunshine of domestic happiness. It changed from the gruesome abode of monkish celibates into a happy Christian home. The Luther union was a happy one. Katie loved her husband and, in return, received his love. Luther declared his love for Katie as follows:

> I would not change my Katie for France and Venice, because God has given her to me, and other women have much worse faults, and she is true to me and a good mother to my children.... The greatest happiness is to have a wife to whom you can trust your business and who is a good mother to your children. Katie, you have a husband who loves you; many an empress is not so well off. I am rich, God has given me my nun and three children: what care I if I am in debt, Katie pays the bills.

It seems that Luther's time was so taken up with the great religious problems of the day, that he gave the business of the household into the hands of his wife. She, being a woman of sound business judgment managed things quite successfully. It is not to be supposed, however, that Luther was ruled by his wife. She seems not to have tried such a thing and doubtless would have failed if she had. Luther says in this respect, "My wife can persuade me anything she pleases, for she has the government of the house in her hands alone. I willingly yield the direction of domestic affairs, but wish my rights to be respected. Women's rule never did any good.... Katie can rule the servants, but not me."

Amid the busy cares and stormy battles of life, Luther found time to enter into the joys and sorrows of his children. Six children came to bless the Luther home. Their names were: Hans, Elizabeth, Magdalene, Martin, Paul, and Margaret. Elizabeth did not live to see her first birthday. Magdalene died when she was thirteen. The death of these two children tore the reformer's heart with grief, because his was the heart of a devoted and true father. Once when Luther was away from home, he wrote the following letter to his little son Hans:

Grace and peace in Christ, dear little son.

I am glad to hear that you are studying and saying your prayers. Continue to do so, my son, and when I come home I will bring you a pretty present.

I know a lovely, pleasant garden where many children are; they wear golden jackets, and gather nice apples under the trees, and pears and cherries, and purple plums and yellow plums, and sing and run and jump and are happy and have pretty little ponies with golden reins and silver saddles. I asked the man who owned the garden who they were. He said, 'They are the children who say their prayers and study and are good.' Then said I, 'Dear man, I also have a son whose name is Hans Luther; may he come into the garden and eat the sweet apples and pears and ride a fine pony and play with these children?' Then the man said, 'If he says his prayers and is good, he may come into the garden and Phil and Justy too, and when they all come they shall have whistles and drums and fifes and shall dance and shoot little crossbows.' Then he showed me a fine, large lawn in the garden for dancing, where hung real golden whistles and fine silver crossbows. But it was yet early, and the children had not finished eating, and I could not wait to see them dance. So I said to the man, 'My dear sir, I must go and write at once to my dear little Hans about all this, so that he will say his prayers and study and be good, so that he may come into the garden, and he has an Auntie Lena whom he must bring with him.' Then the man said, 'All right, go and tell him about it.' So dear little Hans, study and say your prayers, and tell Phil and Justy to say their prayers and study too, so you may all come into the garden together. God bless you. Give Auntie Lena my love and a kiss from me.

Your loving father, Martin Luther.

Handwritten copy of A Mighty Fortress Is Our God

A Mighty Fortress Is Our God

God is our refuge and strength, an ever-present help in trouble. Ps. 46:1

1. A might-y for-tress is our God, a bul-wark nev-er
2. Did we in our own strength con-fide, our striv-ing would be
3. And though this world, with dev-ils filled, should threat-en to un-
4. That Word a-bove all earth-ly pow'rs, no thanks to them, a-

fail - ing; our help-er he a - mid the flood of
los - ing; were not the right man on our side, the
do us, we will not fear, for God hath willed his
bid - eth; the Spir-it and the gifts are ours through

mor - tal ills pre-vail - ing. For still our an - cient foe
man of God's own choos - ing. Dost ask who that may be?
truth to tri - umph through us. The prince of dark - ness grim,
him who with us sid - eth. Let goods and kin - dred go,

doth seek to work us woe; his craft and pow'r are great;
Christ Je - sus, it is he, Lord Sa - ba - oth his name,
we trem - ble not for him; his rage we can en - dure,
this mor - tal life al - so; the bod - y they may kill:

and armed with cru - el hate, on earth is not his e - qual.
from age to age the same, and he must win the bat - tle.
for lo! his doom is sure; one lit - tle word shall fell him.
God's truth a - bid - eth still; his king - dom is for - ev - er.

Based on Psalm 46
Martin Luther, 1529
Tr. by Frederick H. Hedge, 1853

EIN' FESTE BURG 8.7.8.7.6.6.6.6.7.
Martin Luther, 1529

94

Chapter 13

Luther in Death

The last years of Luther's life were rather dismal, and disappointing. Although, like Wesley, a very busy man until the close of life, his greatest work was done a dozen or more years before his death. His life had been so full of battles that old age crept upon him rather prematurely. Ill health had eaten away his physical vitality, but his flaming spirit was not conquered even unto the end. In death he had his same consuming zeal for the truth, and his God still had a mighty hold upon him.

His physical afflictions increased with the years, and at the age of sixty-two, in which year he died, his body was a worn and broken vessel. Not long before his death he wrote,

> Old, decrepit, sluggish, weary, worn out, and now one-eyed, I write to you. Now that I am dead—as I seem to myself—I expect the rest I have deserved to be given me, but instead I am overwhelmed with writing, speaking, transacting business, just as though I had never done, written, said, or accomplished anything.

The shadows of Luther's declining days were deepened by the death of his thirteen-year-old daughter, Magdalene, in 1542. He had regarded her as a most precious treasure, since she had come to bless his home soon after the death of his first daughter, Elizabeth.

Luther's seal

The lion-hearted reformer, which had not been quelled by the fiercest battles that pope and emperor could wage, was melted into tears at the death of his precious child. He felt lonesome. His old friends and associates had moved away or died one by one. He frequently believed that he was going to die and wished that he would. He felt that his work was done, but still he worked on, frequently doing as much work in a month as three ordinary men could do in that time.[†]

But withal, he did not lose his faith in God. A few months before Luther's death, his friend Melanchthon took seriously ill, and it was thought he was dying. Melanchthon lost his speech, became unconscious, and his eyes set. The doctors had given him up to die.

But the staunch old reformer held on to God for him. "O God," said he, "how hadst the devil injured this thy instrument?"

Then to his dear friend, Luther declared, "Be of good cheer, Philip, thou shalt not die."

The sick man whispered, "Do not detain me, for God's sake do not detain me. I am on my way to my eternal rest. Let me depart; nothing better can befall me."

[†] The *Appendix* contains one of Luther's last great works, his *Preface to the Letter of St. Paul to the Romans*, published in 1545.

"No indeed, you must serve God a while yet," answered Luther. He brought food for the sick man, insisted that he eat it, and soon Melanchthon was on the road to recovery.

One day in January 1546, Luther left his Katie, his home, and his friends in Wittenberg. He told them good-bye, and said he would soon return. He never returned alive. He was going to Mansfeld, the scene of his boyhood days, to help settle a dispute between the Counts of Mansfeld. Twice previously, he had gone there on a similar errand. The Counts were brothers, but they had grown to hate each other bitterly. Luther was in too ill health to undertake the trip; but they insisted, so he went, taking their insistence as the voice of duty—a voice to which he never turned a deaf ear. Although hindered by high waters, he reached Eisleben where a council was held and the trouble was settled. Happy at heart over the peace he helped to make, Luther made preparations to return home. He wrote a letter to Katie telling of his intention. He had written many, many letters to his dear Katie—but this was his last:

Eisleben, February 14, 1546.

Grace and peace in the Lord. Dear Katie, we hope to come home this week if God will. God has shown great peace to the lords, who have been reconciled in all but two or three points. It still remains to make them real brothers; this I shall undertake today and shall invite both to visit me, that they may see each other, for hitherto they have not spoken but have embittered each other by writing. But the young lords and the young ladies, too, are happy and make parties for fools' bell and skating, and have masquerades and are all very jolly, even Count Gebhard's son. So we see that God hears prayer.

I send you the trout given me by the Countess Albert. She is heartily happy at this union.

Your little sons are still at Mansfeld.[†] James Luther will take care of them. We eat and drink like lords here and they wait on us so well—too well, indeed, for they might make us forget you at Wittenberg. Moreover, I am no more troubled with the stone. Jonas' leg has become right bad; it is looser on the shin-bone, but God will help it.[††]

You may tell Melanchthon and Bugenhagen and Cruciger everything.

A report has reached here that Dr. Martin Luther has left for Leipzig or Magdeburg. Such tales are invented by those silly wiseacres, your countrymen. Some say the Emperor is thirty miles from here, at Soest in Westphalia; some that the French and the Landgrave of Hesse are raising troops. Let them say and sing; we will wait on God. God bless you.

Dr. Martin Luther.

Luther never wrote any more letters. This one was written February 14. On February 17, he took violent pains in his chest. Hot towels were applied, and he went to bed. He slept until ten o'clock and then awoke in great pain. More hot cloths were brought, and he slept again. About two o'clock, on the morning of the eighteenth, he arose and went into the next room. Here he lay down on a couch. The old house—then an inn—and this room, may still be seen.

Friends hovered near him. Martin and Paul, two of his sons, had hurried from Mansfeld. Hans was not there. Poor Katie was in Wittenberg and could not be

---

† Hans, Martin, and Paul had gone with their father and were visiting at Mansfeld, as Luther transacted his business at Eisleben.

†† Dr. Jonas, who was with Luther at Worms and who was with him on this trip, had hit his leg against a trunk and injured it painfully.

present when her renowned husband passed away. She lived sadly and alone for six years after Luther died. She died and was buried in Torgau in 1552, many miles from Wittenberg, the resting place of her husband.

On that dreary morning of February 18, 1546, those who watched around Luther's bed, as the lion-hearted reformer drew near the silent river, heard him whisper this prayer:

> O my heavenly Father, one God and Father of our Lord Jesus Christ, thou God of all comfort, I thank thee that thou hast given for me thy dear son Jesus Christ, in whom I believe, whom I have preached and confessed, loved and praised. I pray thee, dear Lord Jesus Christ, let me commend my soul to thee. O heavenly Father, if I leave this body and depart I am certain that I will be with thee forever and can never, never tear myself out of thy hands.... Father, into thy hands I commend my spirit. Thou hast redeemed me, thou true God.

Dr. Jonas bowed over him and asked, "Reverend father, will you stand steadfast by Christ and the doctrine you have preached?"

"Yes," was the answer which came distinctly from the dying man's lips. This was his last word. He sank to rest in the arms of the Christ he had so fearlessly preached throughout his stormy career.

On February 19, the funeral procession started its solemn march to Wittenberg, the scene of most of his life's labors. They reached Wittenberg on February 22. Amidst the tolling of bells, the hearse containing the remains of the lion-hearted reformer, followed by his poor widowed Katie, his four orphaned children, and a great host of grief-stricken people, was driven to the castle church. The dead body of Luther was carried through the very door on which, nearly a third of a century before, he had nailed the famous theses. Pastor Bugenhagen, interrupted by his own sobs and those of the people, preached the funeral sermon. Melanchthon, the life-long friend and coworker of Luther, gave an address. The lid of the casket was closed, and it was placed in the vault in the church.

The people returned home wailing, "Luther is dead; Luther is dead." But only the broken and battered house of clay in which he lived was dead. Luther, the real Luther, is alive forevermore and the eternal truths that he preached will never grow old.

Wittenberg, Birthplace of the Protestant Reformation

Appendix

Preface to the Letter of St. Paul to the Romans

by Martin Luther, 1483-1546

Translator's Note:

The material between brackets is explanatory in nature and is not part of Luther's preface. In addition, the terms "just, justice, justify" in this piece are synonymous with the terms "righteous, righteousness, make righteous." Both sets of English words are common translations of the German word *gerecht* and related words. A similar situation exists with the word "faith"; it is synonymous with "belief." Both words can be used to translate the German word *glaube*. Thus, "We are justified by faith" translates the same original German sentence as does "We are made righteous by belief."[†]

[†] Translated by Bro. Andrew Thornton, OSB; "Vorrede auf die Epistel S. Paul: an die Romer" in Dr. Martin Luther's *Die gantze Heilige Schrifft Deudsch 1545 aufs new zurericht*, eds. Hans Volz and Heinz Blanke, vol. 2 (Munich: Roger & Bernhard, 1972), pp. 2254–2268.

Luther's Preface to Romans

This letter is truly the most important piece in the New Testament. It is purest Gospel. It is well worth a Christian's while not only to memorize it word for word but also to occupy himself with it daily, as though it were the daily bread of the soul. It is impossible to read or to meditate on this letter too much or too well. The more one deals with it, the more precious it becomes and the better it tastes. Therefore I want to carry out my service and, with this preface, provide an introduction to the letter, insofar as God gives me the ability, so that everyone can gain the fullest possible understanding of it. Up to now it has been darkened by glosses [explanatory notes and comments which accompany a text] and by many a useless comment, but it is in itself a bright light, almost bright enough to illumine the entire Scripture.

To begin with, we have to become familiar with the vocabulary of the letter and know what St. Paul means by the words *law, sin, grace, faith, justice, flesh, spirit,* etc. Otherwise there is no use in reading it.

You must not understand the word *law* here in human fashion, i.e., a regulation about what sort of works must be done or must not be done. That's the way it is with human laws: you satisfy the demands of the law with works, whether your heart is in it or not. God judges what is in the depths of the heart. Therefore his law also makes demands on the depths of the heart and doesn't let the heart rest content in works; rather it punishes as hypocrisy and lies all works done apart from the depths of the heart. All human beings are called liars (Psalm 116), since none of them keeps or can keep God's law from the depths of the heart. Everyone finds inside himself an aversion to good and a craving for evil. Where there is no free desire for good, there the heart has not set itself on God's law. There also sin is surely to be found and the deserved wrath of God, whether a lot of good works and an honorable life appear outwardly or not.

Therefore in chapter 2, St. Paul adds that the Jews are all sinners and says that only the doers of the law are justified in the sight of God. What he is saying is that no one is a doer of the law by works. On the contrary, he says to them, "You teach that one should not commit adultery, and you commit adultery. You judge another in a certain matter and condemn yourselves in that same matter, because you do the very same thing that you judged in another." It is as if he were saying, "Outwardly you live quite properly in the works of the law and judge those who do not live the same way; you know how to teach everybody. You see the speck in another's eye but do not notice the beam in your own."

Outwardly you keep the law with works out of fear of punishment or love of gain. Likewise you do everything without free desire and love of the law; you act out of aversion and force. You'd rather act otherwise if the law didn't exist. It follows, then, that you, in the depths of your heart, are an enemy of the law. What do you mean, therefore, by teaching another not to steal, when you, in the depths of your heart, are a thief and would be one outwardly too, if you dared. (Of course, outward work doesn't last long with such hypocrites.) So then, you teach others but not yourself; you don't even know what you are teaching. You've never understood the law rightly. Furthermore, the law increases sin, as St. Paul says in chapter 5. That is because a person becomes more and more an enemy of the law the more it demands of him what he can't possibly do.

In chapter 7, St. Paul says, "The law is spiritual." What does that mean? If the law were physical, then it could be satisfied by works, but since it is spiritual, no one can satisfy it unless everything he does springs from the depths of the heart. But no one can give such a heart except the Spirit of God, who makes the person be like the law, so that he actually conceives a heartfelt longing for the law and henceforward does everything, not through fear or coercion, but from a free heart. Such a law is spiritual since it can only be loved and fulfilled by such a heart and such a spirit. If the Spirit is not in the heart, then there remain sin, aversion, and enmity against the law, which in itself is good, just, and holy.

You must get used to the idea that it is one thing to do the works of the law and quite another to fulfill it. The works of the law are everything that a person does or can do of his own free will and by his own powers to obey the law. But because in doing such works the heart abhors the law and yet is forced to obey it, the works are a total loss and are completely useless. That is what St. Paul means in chapter 3 when he says, "No human being is justified before God through the works of the law." From this you can see that the schoolmasters [i.e., the scholastic theologians[†]] and sophists[††] are seducers when they teach that you can prepare yourself for grace by means of works. How can anybody prepare himself for good by means of works if he does no good work except with aversion and constraint in his heart? How can such a work please God, if it proceeds from an averse and unwilling heart?

But to fulfill the law means to do its work eagerly, lovingly and freely, without the constraint of the law; it means to live well and in a manner pleasing to God, as though there were no law or punishment. It is the Holy Spirit, however, who puts such eagerness of unconstrained love into the heart, as Paul says in chapter 5. But the Spirit is given only in, with, and through faith in Jesus Christ, as Paul says in his introduction. So, too, faith comes only through the word of God, the Gospel, that preaches Christ: how he is both Son of God and man, how he died and rose for our sake. Paul says all this in chapters 3, 4, and 10.

That is why faith alone makes someone just and fulfills the law; faith it is that brings the Holy Spirit

---

† Scholastic theologians such as Thomas Aquinas (1225–1274) attempted to reconcile seeming contradictions in revealed truths by reasoning alone. Aquinas' *Summa Theologica* is often regarded as the greatest work of scholasticism. By Luther's time, scholasticism had totally rejected faith, claiming there was no rational ground for it.

†† Sophists were a group of Greek teachers who flourished at the end of the fifth century B.C. They claimed to be purveyors of wisdom—thus, *sophistai*, originally meaning "one who possesses wisdom"—but in reality undertook to show that all true certitude is unattainable. They essentially taught that "man is the measure of all things."

through the merits of Christ. The Spirit, in turn, renders the heart glad and free, as the law demands. Then good works proceed from faith itself. That is what Paul means in chapter 3 when, after he has thrown out the works of the law, he sounds as though the wants to abolish the law by faith. No, he says, we uphold the law through faith, i.e., we fulfill it through faith.

"Sin" in the Scriptures means not only external works of the body but also all those movements within us which bestir themselves and move us to do the external works, namely, the depth of the heart with all its powers. Therefore the word "do" should refer to a person's completely falling into sin. No external work of sin happens, after all, unless a person commit himself to it completely, body and soul. In particular, the Scriptures see into the heart, to the root and main source of all sin—unbelief in the depth of the heart. Thus, even as faith alone makes just and brings the Spirit and the desire to do good external works, so it is only unbelief which sins and exalts the flesh and brings desire to do evil external works. That's what happened to Adam and Eve in Paradise (cf. Genesis 3).

That is why only unbelief is called sin by Christ, as he says in John, chapter 16, "The Spirit will punish the world because of sin, because it does not believe in me." Furthermore, before good or bad works happen, which are the good or bad fruits of the heart, there has to be present in the heart either faith or unbelief, the root, sap, and chief power of all sin. That is why, in the Scriptures, unbelief is called the head of the serpent and of the ancient dragon which the offspring of the woman, i.e., Christ, must crush, as was promised to Adam (cf. Genesis 3). "Grace" and "gift" differ in that grace actually denotes God's kindness or favor which he has toward us and by which he is disposed to pour Christ and the Spirit with His gifts into us, as becomes clear from chapter 5, where Paul says, "Grace and gift are in Christ, etc." The gifts and the Spirit increase daily in us, yet they are not complete, since evil desires and sins remain in us which war against the Spirit, as Paul says in chapter 7, and in Galatians, chapter 5. And Genesis, chapter 3, proclaims the enmity between the offspring of the woman and that of the serpent. But grace does do this much: that we are accounted completely just before God. God's grace is not divided into bits and pieces, as are the gifts, but grace takes us up completely into God's favor for the sake of Christ, our Intercessor and Mediator, so that the gifts may begin their work in us.

In this way, then, you should understand chapter 7, where St. Paul portrays himself as still a sinner, while in chapter 8 he says that, because of the incomplete gifts and because of the Spirit, there is nothing damnable in those who are in Christ. Because our flesh has not been killed, we are still sinners, but because we believe in Christ and have the beginnings of the Spirit, God so shows us his favor and mercy, that he neither notices nor judges such sins. Rather he deals with us according to our belief in Christ until sin is killed.

Faith is not that human illusion and dream that some people think it is. When they hear and talk a lot about faith and yet see that no moral improvement and no good works result from it, they fall into error and say, "Faith is not enough. You must do works if you want to be virtuous and get to heaven." The result is that, when they hear the Gospel, they stumble and make for themselves with their own powers a concept in their hearts which says, "I believe." This concept they hold to be true faith. But since it is a human fabrication and thought and not an experience of the heart, it accomplishes nothing, and there follows no improvement.

Faith is a work of God in us, which changes us and brings us to birth anew from God (cf. John 1). It kills the old Adam, makes us completely different people in heart, mind, senses, and all our powers, and brings the Holy Spirit with it. What a living, creative, active powerful thing is faith! It is impossible for faith to ever stop doing good. Faith doesn't ask whether good works are to be done, but, before it is asked, it has done them. It is always active. Whoever doesn't do such works is without faith; he gropes and searches about him for faith and good works but doesn't know what faith or good works are. Even so, he chatters on with a great many words about faith and good works.

Faith is a living, unshakable confidence in God's grace; it is so certain, that someone would die a thousand times for it. This kind of trust in and knowledge of God's grace makes a person joyful, confident, and happy with regard to God and all creatures. This is what the Holy Spirit does by faith. Through faith, a person will do good to everyone without coercion, willingly and happily; he will serve everyone, suffer everything for the love and praise of God, who has shown him such grace. It is as impossible to separate works from faith as burning and shining from fire. Therefore be on guard against your own false ideas and against the chatterers who think they are clever enough to make judgements about faith and good works but who are in reality the biggest fools. Ask God to work faith in you; otherwise you will remain eternally without faith, no matter what you try to do or fabricate.

Now "justice" is just such a faith. It is called God's justice or that justice which is valid in God's sight, because it is God who gives it and reckons it as justice for the sake of Christ our Mediator. It influences a person to give to everyone what he owes him. Through faith a person becomes sinless and eager for God's commands. Thus he gives God the honor due him and pays him what he owes him. He serves people willingly with the means available to him. In this way he pays everyone his due. Neither nature, nor free will, nor our own powers can bring about such a justice, for even as no one can give himself faith, so too he cannot remove unbelief. How can he then take away even the smallest sin? Therefore everything which takes place outside faith or in unbelief is lie, hypocrisy, and sin (Romans 14), no matter how smoothly it may seem to go.

You must not understand flesh here as denoting only unchastity or spirit as denoting only the inner heart. Here St. Paul calls flesh (as does Christ in John 3) everything born of flesh, i.e., the whole human being with body and soul, reason and senses, since everything in him tends toward the flesh. That is why you should know enough to call that person "fleshly" who—without grace—fabricates, teaches, and chatters about high spiritual matters. You can learn the same thing from Galatians, chapter 5, where St. Paul calls heresy and hatred works of the flesh. And in Romans, chapter 8, he says that, through the flesh, the law is weakened. He says this, not of unchastity, but of all sins, most of all of unbelief, which is the most spiritual of vices.

On the other hand, you should know enough to call that person "spiritual" who is occupied with the most outward of works, as was Christ, when he washed the feet of the disciples, and Peter, when he steered his boat and fished. So then, a person is "flesh" who, inwardly and outwardly, lives only to do those things which are of use to the flesh and to temporal existence. A person is "spirit" who, inwardly and outwardly, lives only to do those things which are of use to the spirit and to the life to come.

Unless you understand these words in this way, you will never understand either this letter of St. Paul or any book of the Scriptures. Be on guard, therefore against any teacher who uses these words differently, no matter who he be, whether Jerome, Augustine, Ambrose, Origen, or anyone else as great as or greater than they. Now let us turn to the letter itself.

The first duty of a preacher of the Gospel is, through his revealing of the law and of sin, to rebuke and to turn into sin everything in life that does not have the Spirit and faith in Christ as its base. Thereby he will lead people to a recognition of their miserable condition, and thus they will become humble and yearn for help. This is what St. Paul does. He begins in chapter 1 by rebuking the gross sins and unbelief which are in plain view, as were (and still are) the sins of the pagans, who live without God's grace. He says that, through the Gospel, God is revealing his wrath from heaven upon all mankind because of the godless and unjust lives they live. For, although they know and recognize day by day that there is a God, yet human nature in itself, without grace, is so evil that it neither thanks nor honors God. This nature blinds itself and continually falls into wickedness, even going so far as to commit idolatry and other horrible sins and vices. It is unashamed of itself and leaves such things unpunished in others.

In chapter 2, St. Paul extends his rebuke to those who appear outwardly pious or who sin secretly. Such were the Jews, and such are all hypocrites still, who live virtuous lives but without eagerness and love; in their heart they are enemies of God's law and like to judge other people. That's the way with hypocrites: they think that they are pure but are actually full of greed, hate, pride, and all sorts of filth (cf. Matthew 23). These are they who despise God's goodness and, by their hardness of heart, heap wrath upon themselves. Thus Paul explains the law rightly when he lets no one remain without sin but proclaims the wrath of God to all who want to live virtuously by nature or by free will. He makes them out to be no better than public sinners; he says they are hard of heart and unrepentant.

In chapter 3, Paul lumps both secret and public sinners together: the one, he says, is like the other; all are sinners in the sight of God. Besides, the Jews had God's word, even though many did not believe in it. But still God's truth and faith in him are not thereby rendered useless. St. Paul introduces, as an aside, the saying from Psalm 51, that God remains true to his words. Then he returns to his topic and proves from Scripture that they are all sinners and that no one becomes just through the works of the law but that God gave the law only so that sin might be perceived.

Next St. Paul teaches the right way to be virtuous and to be saved; he says that they are all sinners, unable to glory in God. They must, however, be justified through faith in Christ, who has merited this for us by his blood and has become for us a mercy seat [cf. Exodus 25:17, Leviticus 16:14ff, and John 2:2] in the presence of God, who forgives us all our previous sins. In so doing, God proves that it is his justice alone, which he gives through faith, that helps us, the justice which was at the appointed time revealed through the Gospel and, previous to that, was witnessed to by the Law and the Prophets. Therefore the law is set up by faith, but the works of the law, along with the glory taken in them, are knocked down by faith. [As with the term "spirit," the word "law" seems to have for Luther, and for St. Paul, two meanings. Sometimes it means "regulation about what must be done or not done," as in the third paragraph of this preface; sometimes it means "the Torah," as in the previous sentence. And sometimes it seems to have both meanings, as in what follows.]

In chapters 1 to 3, St. Paul has revealed sin for what it is and has taught the way of faith which leads to justice. Now in chapter 4 he deals with some objections and criticisms. He takes up first the one raised by people who—on hearing that faith makes just without works—say, "What? Shouldn't we do any good works?" Here St. Paul holds up Abraham as an example. He says, "What did Abraham accomplish with his good works? Were they all good for nothing and useless?" He concludes that Abraham was made righteous apart from all his works by faith alone. Even before the "work" of his circumcision, Scripture praises him as being just on account of faith alone (cf. Genesis 15). Now if the work of his circumcision did nothing to make him just, a work that God had commanded him to do and hence a work of obedience, then surely no other good work can do anything to make a person just. Even as Abraham's circumcision was an outward sign with which he proved his justice based on faith, so too all good works are only outward signs which flow from faith and are the fruits of faith; they prove that the person is already inwardly just in the sight of God.

St. Paul verifies his teaching on faith in chapter 3 with a powerful example from Scripture. He calls as witness David, who says in Psalm 32 that a person becomes just without works but doesn't remain without works once he has become just. Then Paul extends this example and applies it against all other works of the law. He concludes that the Jews cannot be Abraham's heirs just because of their blood relationship to him and still less because of the works of the law. Rather, they have to inherit Abraham's faith if they want to be his real heirs, since it was prior to the Law of Moses and the law of circumcision that Abraham became just through faith and was called a father of all believers. St. Paul adds that the law brings about more wrath than grace, because no one obeys it with love and eagerness. More disgrace than grace come from the works of the law. Therefore faith alone can obtain the grace promised to Abraham. Examples like these are written for our sake, that we also should have faith.

In chapter 5, St. Paul comes to the fruits and works of faith, namely: joy, peace, love for God and for all people; in addition: assurance, steadfastness, confidence, courage, and hope in sorrow and suffering. All of these follow where faith is genuine, because of the overflowing good will that God has shown in Christ: he had him die for us before we could ask him for it, yes, even while we were still his enemies. Thus, when God has established true faith, without any good works, God makes men just. It does not follow from that, however, that we should not do good works; rather it means that morally upright works do not remain lacking. About such works the "works-holy" people know nothing;

they invent for themselves their own works in which are neither peace, nor joy, nor assurance, nor love, nor hope, nor steadfastness, nor any kind of genuine Christian works or faith.

Next St. Paul makes a digression, a pleasant little side-trip, and relates where both sin and justice, death and life come from. He [plays off] these two: Adam and Christ. What he wants to say is that Christ, a second Adam, had to come in order to make us heirs of his justice through a new spiritual birth in faith, just as the old Adam made us heirs of sin through the old fleshy birth.

St. Paul proves, by this reasoning, that a person cannot help himself by his works to get from sin to justice any more than he can prevent his own physical birth. St. Paul also proves that the divine law, which should have been well-suited, if anything was, for helping people to obtain justice, not only was no help at all when it did come, but it even increased sin. Evil human nature, consequently, becomes more hostile to it; the more the law forbids it to indulge its own desires, the more it wants to. Thus the law makes Christ all the more necessary and demands more grace to help human nature.

In chapter 6, St. Paul takes up the special work of faith, the struggle which the spirit wages against the flesh to kill off those sins and desires that remain after a person has been made just. He teaches us that faith doesn't so free us from sin that we can be idle, lazy, and self-assured, as though there were no more sin in us. Sin "is" there, but, because of faith that struggles against it, God does not reckon sin as deserving damnation. Therefore we have in our own selves a lifetime of work cut out for us; we have to tame our body, kill its lusts, force its members to obey the spirit and not the flesh. We must do this so that we may conform to the death and resurrection of Christ and complete our Baptism, which signifies a death to sin and a new life of grace. Our aim is to be completely clean from sin and then to rise bodily with Christ and live forever.

St. Paul says that we can accomplish all this because we are in grace and not in the law. He explains that to be "outside the law" is not the same as having no law and being able to do what you please. No, being "under the law" means living without grace, surrounded by the works of the law. Then surely sin reigns by means of the law, since no one is naturally well-disposed toward the law. That very condition, however, is the greatest sin. But grace makes the law lovable to us, so there is then no sin any more, and the law is no longer against us but one with us.

This is true freedom from sin and from the law; St. Paul writes about this for the rest of the chapter. He says it is a freedom only to do good with eagerness and to live a good life without the coercion of the law. This freedom is, therefore, a spiritual freedom which does not suspend the law but which supplies what the law demands, namely eagerness and love. These silence the law so that it has no further cause to drive people on and make demands of them. It's as though you owed something to a moneylender and couldn't pay him. You could be rid of him in one of two ways: either he would take nothing from you and would tear up his account book, or a pious man would pay for you and give you what you needed to satisfy your debt. That's exactly how Christ freed us from the law. Therefore our freedom is not a wild, fleshy freedom that has no obligation to do anything. On the contrary, it is a freedom that does a great deal, indeed everything, yet is free of the law's demands and debts.

In chapter 7, St. Paul confirms the foregoing by an analogy drawn from married life. When a man dies, the wife is free; the one is free and clear of the other. It is not the case that the woman may not or should not marry another man; rather she is now for the first time free to marry someone else. She could not do this before she was free of her first husband. In the same way, our conscience is bound to the law so long as our condition is that of the sinful old man. But when the old man is killed by the spirit, then the conscience is free, and conscience and law are [freed] of each other. Not that conscience should now do nothing; rather, it should now for the first time truly cling to its second husband, Christ, and bring forth the fruit of life.

Next St. Paul sketches further the nature of sin and the law. It is the law that makes sin really active and powerful, because the old man gets more and more hostile to the law since he can't pay the debt demanded by the law. Sin is his very nature; of himself he can't do otherwise. And so the law is his death and torture. Now the law is not itself evil; it is our evil nature that cannot tolerate that the good law should demand good from it. It's like the case of a sick person, who cannot tolerate that you demand that he run and jump around and do other things that a healthy person does.

St. Paul concludes here that, if we understand the law properly and comprehend it in the best possible way, then we will see that its sole function is to remind us of our sins, to kill us by our sins, and to make us deserving of eternal wrath. Conscience learns and experiences all this in detail when it comes face-to-face with the law. It follows, then, that we must have something else, over and above the law, which can make a person virtuous and cause him to be saved. Those, however, who do not understand the law rightly are blind; they go their way boldly and think they are satisfying the law with works. They don't know how much the law demands, namely, a free, willing, eager heart. That is the reason that they don't see Moses rightly before their eyes. [In both Jewish and Christian teaching, Moses was commonly held to be the author of the Pentateuch, the first five books of the Bible. Compare the involved imagery of Moses' face and the veil over it in 2 Corinthians 3:7–18.] For them he is covered and concealed by the veil.

The Glory of the New Covenant
2 Corinthians 3: 7–18 (NKJV)

Now if the ministry that brought death, which was engraved in letters on stone, came with glory, so that the Israelites could not look steadily at the face of Moses because of its glory, fading though it was, will not the ministry of the Spirit be even more glorious? If the ministry that condemns men is glorious, how much more glorious is the ministry that brings righteousness! For what was glorious has no glory now in comparison with the surpassing glory. And if what was fading away came with glory, how much greater is the glory of that which lasts!

Therefore, since we have such a hope, we are very bold. We are not like Moses, who would put a veil over his face to keep the Israelites from gazing at it while the radiance was fading away. But their minds were made dull, for to this day the same veil remains when the old covenant is read. It has not been removed, because only in Christ is it taken away. Even to this day when Moses is read, a veil covers their hearts. But whenever anyone turns to the Lord, the veil is taken away. Now the Lord is the Spirit, and where the Spirit of the Lord is, there is freedom. And we, who with unveiled faces all reflect the Lord's glory, are being transformed into his likeness with ever-increasing glory, which comes from the Lord, who is the Spirit.

Then St. Paul shows how spirit and flesh struggle with each other in one person. He gives himself as an example, so that we may learn how to kill sin in ourselves. He gives both spirit and flesh the name "law," so that, just as it is in the nature of divine law to drive a person on and make demands of him, so too the flesh drives and demands and rages against the spirit and wants to have its own way. Likewise the spirit drives and demands against the flesh and wants to have its own way. This feud lasts in us for as long as we live, in one person more, in another less, depending on whether spirit or flesh is stronger. Yet the whole human being is both—spirit and flesh. The human being fights with himself until he becomes completely spiritual.

In chapter 8, St. Paul comforts fighters such as these and tells them that this flesh will not bring them condemnation. He goes on to show what the nature of flesh and spirit are. Spirit, he says, comes from Christ, who has given us his Holy Spirit; the Holy Spirit makes us spiritual and restrains the flesh. The Holy Spirit assures us that we are God's children no matter how furiously sin may rage within us, so long as we follow the Spirit and struggle against sin in order to kill it. Because nothing is so effective in deadening the flesh as the cross and suffering, Paul comforts us in our suffering. He says that the Spirit, [cf. previous note about the meaning of "spirit"] love and all creatures will stand by us; the Spirit in us groans and all creatures long with us that we be freed from the flesh and from sin. Thus we see that these three chapters, 6, 7, and 8, all deal with the one work of faith, which is to kill the old Adam and to constrain the flesh.

In chapters 9, 10, and 11, St. Paul teaches us about the eternal providence of God. It is the original source which determines who would believe and who would not, who can be set free from sin and who cannot. Such matters have been taken out of our hands and are put into God's hands so that we might become virtuous. It is absolutely necessary that it be so, for we are so weak and unsure of ourselves that, if it depended on us, no human being would be saved. The devil would overpower all of us. But God is steadfast; his providence will not fail, and no one can prevent its realization. Therefore we have hope against sin.

But here we must shut the mouths of those sacrilegious and arrogant spirits who, mere beginners that they are, bring their reason to bear on this matter and commence, from their exalted position, to probe the abyss of divine providence and uselessly trouble themselves about whether they are predestined or not. These people must surely plunge to their ruin, since they will either despair or abandon themselves to a life of chance.

You, however, follow the reasoning of this letter in the order in which it is presented. Fix your attention first of all on Christ and the Gospel, so that you may recognize your sin and His grace. Then struggle against sin, as chapters 1–8 have taught you to. Finally, when you have come, in chapter 8, under the shadow of the cross and suffering, they will teach you, in chapters 9–11, about providence and what a comfort it is. [The context here and in St. Paul's letter makes it clear that this is the cross and passion, not only of Christ, but of each Christian.] Apart from suffering, the cross and the pangs of death, you cannot come to grips with providence without harm to yourself and secret anger against God. The old Adam must be quite dead before you can endure this matter and drink this strong wine. Therefore make sure you don't drink wine while you are still a babe at the breast. There is a proper measure, time and age for understanding every doctrine.

In chapter 12, St. Paul teaches the true liturgy and makes all Christians priests, so that they may offer, not money or cattle, as priests do in the Law, but their own bodies, by putting their desires to death. Next he describes the outward conduct of Christians whose lives are governed by the Spirit; he tells how they teach, preach, rule, serve, give, suffer, love, live, and act toward friend, foe, and everyone. These are the works that a Christian does, for, as I have said, faith is not idle.

In chapter 13, St. Paul teaches that one should honor and obey the secular authorities. He includes this, not because it makes people virtuous in the sight of God, but because it does insure that the virtuous have outward peace and protection and that the wicked cannot do evil without fear and in undisturbed peace. Therefore it is the duty of virtuous people to honor secular authority, even though they do not, strictly speaking, need it. Finally, St. Paul sums up everything in love and gathers it all into the example of Christ: what he has done for us, we must also do and follow after him.

In chapter 14, St. Paul teaches that one should carefully guide those with weak conscience and spare them. One shouldn't use Christian freedom to harm but rather to help the weak. Where that isn't done, there follow dissension and despising of the Gospel, on which everything else depends. It is better to give way a little to the weak in faith until they become stronger than to have the teaching of the Gospel perish completely. This work is a particularly necessary work of love especially now when people, by eating meat and by other freedoms, are brashly, boldly, and unnecessarily shaking weak consciences which have not yet come to know the truth.

In chapter 15, St. Paul cites Christ as an example to show that we must also have patience with the weak, even those who fail by sinning publicly or by their disgusting morals. We must not cast them aside but must bear with them until they become better. That is the way Christ treated us and still treats us every day; He puts up with our vices, our wicked morals and all our imperfection, and He helps us ceaselessly. Finally, Paul prays for the Christians at Rome; he praises them and commends them to God. He points out his own office and the message that he preaches. He makes an unobtrusive plea for a contribution for the poor in Jerusalem. Unalloyed love is the basis of all he says and does.

The last chapter consists of greetings. But Paul also includes a salutary warning against human doctrines which are preached alongside the Gospel and which do a great deal of harm. It's as though he had clearly seen that out of Rome and through the Romans would come the deceitful, harmful Canons and Decretals[†] along with the entire brood and swarm of human laws and commands that is now drowning the whole world and has blotted out this letter and the whole of the Scriptures, along with the Spirit and faith. Nothing remains but the idol Belly, and St. Paul depicts those people here as its servants. God deliver us from them. Amen.

---

† Early church law developed particularly from the canons of church councils and from the letters of bishops regarding church discipline and governance. The Church of Rome later expanded canon law by adding papal letters, called *decretals*, which settle matters of ecclesiastical government and discipline. Today papal decrees are called Canons and Decretals, not laws.

We find in this letter, then, the richest possible teaching about what a Christian should know: the meaning of law, Gospel, sin, punishment, grace, faith, justice, Christ, God, good works, love, hope and the cross. We learn how we are to act toward everyone, toward the virtuous and sinful, toward the strong and the weak, friend and foe, and toward ourselves. Paul bases everything firmly on Scripture and proves his points with examples from his own experience and from the Prophets, so that nothing more could be desired. Therefore it seems that St. Paul, in writing this letter, wanted to compose a summary of the whole of Christian and evangelical teaching which would also be an introduction to the whole Old Testament. Without doubt, whoever takes this letter to heart possesses the light and power of the Old Testament. Therefore each and every Christian should make this letter the habitual and constant object of his study. God grant us his grace to do so. Amen.

*This translation of Luther's **Vorrede** to Romans was made by Bro. Andrew Thornton, OSB, for the Saint Anselm College Humanities Program.*